I thank the many people who have provided me with information and suggestions that made this book possible. Most of them have asked that their names not be published. They have not. Others declined to identify themselves so I do not even know who they are.

DON'T BUG ME

ME

THE LATEST HIGH-TECH SPY METHODS

M.L. Shannon

PALADIN PRESS
BOULDER, COLORADO

Don't Bug Me:
The Latest High-Tech Spy Methods
by M.L. Shannon

Copyright © 1992 by M.L. Shannon

ISBN 0-87364-658-4
Printed in the United States of America

Published by Paladin Press, a division of
Paladin Enterprises, Inc., P.O. Box 1307,
Boulder, Colorado 80306, USA.
(303) 443-7250

Direct inquires and/or orders to the above address.

CONTENTS

"Sed quis custodiet ipsos Custodes?" ("But who is to guard the guards themselves?")

Juvenal (ca. 50 — 130 A.D.)
Satires

WARNING

This book contains a considerable amount of information about surveillance methods and equipment, some of which has never been published.

It is intended as a manual for self-defense against eavesdroppers. I do not encourage anyone to use it to invade the privacy of any other person. Bugging people is against several laws. It could get you arrested and put in a place you wouldn't like very much.

The author and the publisher are not responsible for the use or misuse of any information contained in this book.

INTRODUCTION

I believe that everyone in America should be allowed to enjoy the right guaranteed by the Fourth Amendment: the right to be left alone by government and others who would invade their privacy. I believe this, but not everyone else does.

There are many people in this country—and not just federal agents—who can listen to everything you and your family are saying in your home, on your telephones, or in your office or car. They can and sometimes do. I think that everyone has the right to know about this.

Information about the methods, types of equipment, easy availability, effectiveness, and means to find and defeat them should be available to everyone who wants it.

People are entitled to get what they bargained for when they place their security, peace of mind, and their cash (usually a lot of the last) in the hands of someone who claims he can make their homes and offices secure from spies and wiretappers.

SURVEILLANCE AND ETHICS

Bugging people may be unlawful, but it is not always morally wrong, e.g., when a person is being victimized by another and law-enforcement agencies are unable or unwilling to help. Bugging should be used only in self-defense. There are no "Equalizers" and "A-Teams" in real life.

The guy was a real lowlife, very big and very mean, and he had a lot of friends. Everyone who frequented the bar was afraid of him, especially the bartender, who was his ex-wife. He would come into the bar drunk and force her to go with him on his motorcycle. Sometimes he would beat her, and when she came back to work, everyone saw her bruised, puffy face.

She called his military commanding officer, but he told her that without evidence or witnesses, there was nothing he could do.

She called the police, who said they would "drive by" and look for him, but they could never catch him at the tavern.

One of the bar regulars was an electronics technician, who, after seeing her abused once too often, told her he might be able to help. He built a bug, showed her how to turn it on, and suggested some hiding places for it. The next time her ex-husband forced her to go with him, she hid the bug in his bedroom.

For ten nights the technician parked his old Dodge van near the guy's apartment and listened until he got something he could use: the sounds of him verbally abusing and then beating another woman he had taken home.

The next day, he made copies of the tape and sent one to the guy, along with a note, and another to his CO. The ex never came back to the bar again. This is a true story.

I understand the helplessness law-enforcement officials must feel when arrested drug dealers and other criminals are back on the street within hours; I sympathize with them if they bend the rules to try to keep known criminals off the street. I don't like crime either.

What I do not sympathize with is the government's abuse of the power it has to spy on people who are not criminals and are not even suspected of a crime, such as political activists and protestors who disagree with the way the administration is running the country. This I am against.

When Richard Nixon had Assistant U.S. Attorney General Morton Halperin's phones tapped, was there a clear and present danger to national security to justify this action? Nixon remarked of this: "When a president does it, it is not illegal."

During the Nixon administration, federal agents tapped the phones of those they believed to be political dissidents, and U.S. Attorney General John Mitchell tried to justify this by claiming that "national security may involve threats from domestic groups."

The U.S. Supreme Court disagreed with Mitchell, and ruled that the government could not indiscriminately tap the phones of suspected dissidents.

The Federal Bureau of Investigation (FBI) has, for years, tried to get public libraries to provide the names of patrons who check out certain books that it considers seditious, and agents have admitted that they go to libraries to look for people who read publications such as Aviation Week, Defense Electronics, and other technical magazines. Is reading a magazine that anyone can subscribe to a threat to national security?

A few years ago, the FBI conducted a large-scale surveillance operation against members of a group of people who were protesting the United States' involvement in El Salvador, and the agency got caught doing this. The punishment for the agents involved in violating surveillance laws was not a long prison term, as the laws specify, but rather a short suspension without pay.

There are people who spy on others for selfish, malicious reasons or, sometimes, for apparent reasons other than the fact that they have the opportunity. The following is one such example.

Sylvia was a popular girl; she was pretty, sweet, innocent, friendly, and trusting. She was twenty-two, had a job she liked, and enjoyed her bit parts in the musicals at a local open-air theater. She had a lot going for her, but apparently someone didn't like her.

Strange things kept happening to her. She called a friend and arranged to meet her at a shopping center. When she got back to her car, she found that someone had let the air out of the tires. Another time she made a date to go to a movie, but the guy called to tell her that someone had broken his windshield, and he was unable to take her because he was too upset. On another occasion, she called a taxi, but after waiting for a long time and then calling to check on it, she was told that someone had cancelled it. Too many strange things were happening, and it distressed her.

One day a friend whom Sylvia confided in suggested that maybe someone was listening in on her telephone. This was even more distressing—she was so naive that she couldn't believe anyone would do that. This friend knew a guy from high school who was in the school radio club and known as an electronics kook. She called him and asked if he knew how someone could listen in on someone's telephone.

He knew a little bit about phone tapping, and he agreed to look at Sylvia's phone line. In just a few minutes, he found a wire connected to her line in the basement. He traced it to a line going to another apartment, and they called the police and the phone company. The police arrested the man who lived in that apartment. Sylvia was there when the police took the man away; she didn't even know him.

• • •

I am against using surveillance for selfish or malicious purposes. I know what it is like to be bugged.

A SPECULATIVE HISTORY OF SPYING

Sir William Blackstone defined eavesdroppers as, "Such as listen under walls or windows, or the eaves of a house, to harken after discourse, and thereupon to frame slanderous and mischievous tales."

Surveillance is as old as man. Supreme Court Justice Hugo L. Black observed of it that "the practice has undoubtedly gone on since the beginning of human society."

Even when our distant ancestors were living in caves, there were probably those who liked to spy on others—to see where they hid their food, to watch caveman with cavewoman, or just because they were nosey.

As the spoken language developed, some person probably discovered, man being a curious and inventive creature, that he could hear better by listening through a hollow reed or other such organic listening device; maybe a coconut shell was the original "contact microphone."

Speaking led to a way of recording what people had to say, the written language. At first, it was the exclusive property of kings and courts, the rich and powerful. Common people were forbidden from having books or knowing how to read them, sometimes under penalty of death by torture.

Hundreds of years passed before the peasants were allowed this knowledge, but the heads of state still didn't like the idea.

They had secrets they didn't want the people to read, but there were plenty of people who were determined to read. Government officials started to worry, and they developed codes to hide information from citizens who could now read.

One of the earliest of these was the "Caesar Cipher," which was a simple letter substitution like the cryptograms in newspapers. The Spartan code involved writing the message on a strip of cloth wound around a specific-size spear, then removing it. Only by rewrapping it on something the same size as the spear could it be read. Other codes had interesting names such as the Russian "Nihilist" and "Prisoner" codes, the "Corkscrew," "Rail Fence," "Spaghetti," and "Swinging Squares."

Codes were broken; new ones were devised and subsequently broken; locks were invented, followed closely by picks; and spying continued.

The earliest likely example of electronic spying was in the Old West, where outlaw gangs used stolen telegraphs and tapped the lines to find out what the sheriff was up to or the date of the next gold shipment. While no one knows for sure who the first telephone tapper was, it could have been Watson.

Soon the American Telephone and Telegraph Company was born, with its operator-assisted calls. But it was too easy for the operators to listen in, believed an undertaker named Strowger, so in 1889 he invented the mechanical "stepping switch" that automatically connected the lines, and the manual switchboards were replaced. This kept the operators from listening, but it was still easy for anyone else to tap a phone line.

In December 1947 Drs. Bardeen, Shockley, and Brattain, working at Bell Laboratories, invented the transistor, and the age of modern surveillance was born.

Today there are many high-tech methods of spying on others, and it has become big business—governments spend billions of dollars for satellites and supercomputers, microwave equipment, sophisticated bugs, lasers, and all types of other devices to spy on other governments and the American people. Industrial espionage has become a big business in itself, and easily available, low-cost surveillance devices have made it more common for people to spy on other people.

Knowledge has not kept up with the technology, at least not in terms of the general public's knowing how to counter electronic invasion by others. Anyone can buy a wireless microphone and use it to spy on someone else, but it's not easy to find a book that tells how to stop bugging or how to find a hidden listening device.

You won't find these books at Waldenbooks or B. Dalton, and they are not book-of-the month selections. The few listed in libraries' card catalogues are usually "missing" (checked out and not returned). This partly explains why people know so little about spying and countermeasures.

YOUR RIGHT TO KNOW

While researching this book, I went to several shopping malls with a tape recorder and notebook and asked people if they knew anything about spying, surveillance, and wiretapping. I got a lot of strange looks from people who hurried away as if I were maybe a spy or something. (Of course, maybe the black fedora, trench coat, and sunglasses had something to do with this.) I saw obvious anger in some faces, and one man replied, "Yeah, the government spies on all of us." But by far the most common reaction was a blank stare and a comment like, "Oh, well, not much. I never really thought about it."

People are still unsuspecting in an age where surveillance is so easy. Perhaps if they knew how easy it is to spy on others they would care, and if they knew that they can do a great deal to prevent being spied upon, they would want to know how.

This book is for everyone. It assumes that the reader knows very little about surveillance and presents information about different methods of eaves-dropping, types of spying equipment available and how they are used and countered, and, finally, how to buy, build, and use some of these devices.

I like to think I have included at least a little information on every method of surveillance that exists, but there may well be equipment or methods I know nothing about. I would like to hear from anyone who does. Anonymous letters in care of the publisher (Paladin Press, P.O. Box 1307, Boulder, CO 80306) are welcome.

Finally, although this book is intended for everyone, each person's situation is unique. Some people are more likely to be bugged than others. Different people react to spying in different ways, and people have to decide for themselves how far they are willing to go to prevent their being bugged.

This book doesn't have all of the answers for every situation, but it has enough basic information to enable readers to know how to deal with the possibility of being bugged, protect themselves against it, and relate to professional debuggers on their own terms.

THE TRUTH ABOUT COUNTERSURVEILLANCE

There are people who claim to be countersurveillance experts and who are happy to take your money in exchange for sweeping your home or office for bugs. Most really are experts, but a few are not. Most are well-equipped; a few aren't. This book will help you tell one from the other.

You can start to separate the real pros from the wannabes by asking a few questions. Ask if they have a bug detector that will cover the low- and medium-frequency bands, or if they use a spectrum analyzer. Ask them about down-line phone taps and how they would look for them. Anyone who knows his business will not be offended by such questions. Remarked one private investigator who resented my comments after he said he could find any kind of surveillance, including an inductive down-line wiretap, "Who are you to question me, anyway? I have been in this business for twenty years, and I . . ." Another person who told me he did counter-surveillance work didn't know what a nonlinear junction detector was.

There are established companies with experienced experts in the field listed in the yellow pages under "security consultants." I would start with them rather than someone who does debugging as a sideline.

Some methods of spying on people cannot be detected by any electronic countersurveillance equipment; others are difficult to find. Most, however, are simple to find. The real experts will tell you this. There are no methods of electronic surveillance that I know of against which you are totally helpless. Even if there is no way to detect some of them with electronic equipment, all can be dealt with and defeated. It may be inconvenient, and it may be expensive, but it can be done. You *can* protect yourself from electronic surveillance.

But remember, if you believe you are being bugged and decide to call in a team of counter-surveillance experts, make the call from a pay phone. Don't let a spy know you suspect him.

WHY ME?

"Why would anyone want to bug me?" some of you are probably asking. Are you "important" enough to place under surveillance? What is important to some people isn't to others. You don't have to be rich or famous, a public figure, criminal, or political activist to be on someone's watch list—although it does help.

A small contractor preparing a bid on a small job can be a target. If a competing company knows what the competition is prepared to bid, it can bid lower. This is one way that small companies become large companies. A jealous spouse with twenty dollars can buy a wireless microphone and make you a target. One business partner thinks the other is cheating him, so he bugs him. Law firms bug opposition firms more often than people think because it never makes the newspapers. A neighbor bugs another neighbor because of some petty misunderstanding. Students bug teachers to get test information. Management bugs employees to find out what's going on or what they think. Strangers bug strangers just for the hell of it. The federal government has been known to bend the rules a little when they want to spy on someone. How many of these categories do you fall into?

In the several years I spent gathering information for this book, I interviewed dozens of people in dozens of cities. The interviewees included counter-surveillance experts, debugging equipment manufacturers or vendors, law-enforcement personnel, former federal agents, lawyers, phone company employees, electronic technicians and engineers, victims of surveillance, and a few who had bugged others.

Big Business Is Biggest Offender

One conclusion their testimonies and other information I gathered make clear is that most illegal bugging is done by big businesses spying on each other or their employees.

Surveillance by the Federal Government

On the other hand, illegal surveillance by the feds appears to be less common than I (and most people) imagined. (But still not uncommon enough.) There are two apparent reasons for this. First, most surveillance is illegal, and if a federal agent gets caught conducting an illegal surveillance, he might lose his job (a job that could be very well-paying). Chances are, he would get off with a series of reprimands, but there are limits to what federal employees can get away with.

Second, surveillances are expensive. Who is going to pay for the equipment? While most federal agents have access to surveillance gear, they have to account for it, and once a bug is installed, it generally stays installed. You don't usually get it back, and quality bugs are not cheap.

Then, once installed, someone has to be in place to hear what the device is receiving. Unless it is a high-powered and expensive repeater system, that means setting up a listening post—usually in a van with agents to man it. To be effective, this has to be continuous. If an agent leaves for a short time, he may miss the information he is listening for. Stakeouts of this type can take a lot of time.

Finally, while the information received in this way may be extremely useful, it cannot be used as evidence in court.

Federal agents do conduct unlawful surveillance—they have been caught doing so—but it's not like they can bug anyone, anytime.

Of the People and by the People

Personal surveillance by ordinary people is more common than one might think. Bugs are easy to get and use, and the average person is totally defenseless against them.

Many buggers are close enough to the people they bug that they can access areas they want to bug without breaking in. These include friends, neighbors, and family members. With the same access, they can usually retrieve the bug when it has served its purpose, so it is never found and there is no record of it.

Even when a person or a business discovers that surveillance has been going on, the public rarely hears about it because he or it doesn't tell anyone. No one wants that kind of publicity.

Regardless of who is bugging whom, and how often, there are many who are concerned about it. At the end of this book is a list of companies that sell equipment used for surveillance or counter-surveillance devices. There are more than forty businesses on it, and it is far from complete. For local vendors, look in the yellow pages under "security consultants." In a large city, there are a number of them listed, and these businesses are surviving, even thriving, even though the cost of sweeping an office for bugs is considerable, and the equipment is not cheap. People are paying this money for equipment or expertise because there is a need for it.

One of the professional debuggers we talked to made an interesting comment: "You look in the back of any of a number of magazines, electronics and like that, and you see ads for wireless microphones and phone bugs and that stuff. This has been going on for forty years, and if they weren't selling these things, they wouldn't keep running the ads." Someone is buying them.

THE LAWS THAT CONCERN SURVEILLANCE

This chapter is not intended as legal advice. It simply points out that there are laws against people bugging other people. The Omnibus Crime Control and Safe Streets Act of 1968, which breezed through Congress (368 to 17 in the House and 72 to 4 in the Senate), was intended as a tool to fight organized crime. For the first time, this bill made it legal for the government to "intercept wire and oral communications under specified conditions, with safeguards designed to protect the right of privacy," and it made it unlawful for people to do the same thing. "Specified conditions" were defined as a court order or a situation that was a matter of "national security."

The Omnibus Act reads in part:

"(1) *Except as otherwise specifically provided in this chapter any person who:*

(a) willfully intercepts, endeavors to intercept, or procures any other person to intercept or endeavor to intercept, any wire or oral communication;

(b) willfully uses, endeavors to use, or procures any other person to use or endeavor to use any electronic, mechanical, or other device to intercept any oral communication when

(i) such device is affixed to, or otherwise transmits a signal through, a wire, cable, or other like connection used in wire communication; or

(ii) such device transmits communications by radio, or interferes with the transmission of such communication; or

(iii) such person knows, or has reason to know, that such device or any component thereof has been sent through the mail or transported in interstate or foreign commerce; or

(iv) such use or endeavor to use

(A) takes place on the premises of any business or other commercial establishment the operations of which affect interstate or foreign commerce; or

(B) obtains or is for the purpose of obtaining information relating to the operations of any business or other commercial establishment the operations of which affect interstate or foreign commerce; or

(v) such person acts in the District of Columbia, the Commonwealth of Puerto Rico, or any territory or possession of the United States;

(c) willfully discloses, or endeavors to disclose, to any other person the contents of any wire or oral communication, knowing or having reason to know that the information was obtained through the interception of a wire or oral communication in violation of this subsection; or

(d) willfully uses, or endeavors to use, the contents of any wire or oral communication, knowing or having reason to know that the information was obtained through the interception of a wire or oral communication in violation of this subsection;

shall be fined not more than $10,000.00 or imprisoned not more than five years, or both."

The act goes on to say that agents, switchboard operators, and employees working in the normal course of their employment with a communication common carrier, the FCC, and telephone operators who are "making mechanical or service quality-control checks" are exempt from this law.

Also exempt is anyone acting for the president as a matter of national security. This law specifically states, "Nothing contained in the act or in section 605 of the Communications Act of 1934 shall limit the constitutional power of the President to take such measures as he deems necessary to protect the Nation against a clear and present danger to the structure or existence of the Government."

What this part of Omnibus seems to say is that:

• It is legal for the government agencies to bug people if they have a warrant or if the situation concerns national security—or if they don't get caught.

• It is against the law for people to bug people by using any kind of device that is attached to a wire or transmits a radio signal or has been transported through foreign or interstate commerce.

Since practically everything that could be used as a surveillance device is made—at least in part—in Japan, Taiwan, or Singapore, this would apparently include wireless microphones and other RF transmitters, shotgun microphones, lasers, and, in fact, virtually any method of eavesdropping except hiding "in the eaves of a house."

Section 2512 of this long, complicated law, states:

"Any person who willfully sends through the mail, or sends or carries any electronic, mechanical, or other device, knowing or having reason to know that the design of such device renders it primarily useful for the purpose of the surreptitious interception of wire or oral communications, or knows or has reason to know that such advertisement will be sent

through the mail or transferred interstate shall be fined no more than $10,000.00 or imprisoned not more than five years or both."

In general, this section seems to say that it is unlawful to make, sell, advertise, ship, or use surveillance devices that are "primarily useful" for spying on people. But where does it say anything about possessing such devices?

Wireless microphones are used more often than any other type of transmitter, and anyone can buy one. There are kits that when assembled are wireless microphones and telephone line transmitters, whose purchase or ownership is either legal (but whose sale is still illegal) or is not being enforced by the law.

Apparently, possession is not considered sufficient to constitute an "endeavor to unlawfully use"; if it were, then every person who owns a wireless microphone, baby monitor, or two-way radio would be violating the law.

The bottom line, as someone who claimed to be a former federal agent told us, is if federal officials wanted to, they could arrest anyone who owns anything that could be used for surveillance. Such is the power given to the government over the people by this act.

Although not everyone arrested and charged under this law would be convicted, most people would be bankrupted by the legal cost of a trial in U.S. District Court. But as there are so many places that sell phone tap kits and wireless microphones, it would also be prohibitively expensive to the government to locate, arrest, and try all of them.

To help control this problem, the Federal Communications Commission (FCC), or someone pretending to represent it, is getting into the act. All devices that transmit an RF signal have to be "type accepted" by the FCC, and this costs several thousand dollars for each model. The FCC has sent letters to companies that make these kits, according to an article in *Full Disclosure*.

Public Law 99-508 (the Electronic Communications Privacy Act of 1986, Title 18 USC, various sections) also concerns surveillance. It says (in part) that there are some kinds of radio telephone calls and radio transmissions that are legal to listen to and some that are illegal. This is discussed in more detail later.

In addition to federal laws, there are local laws against surveillance breaking and entering, unlawful entry, trespassing, and invasion of privacy.

Ultimately, however, the law is whatever the Supreme Court says it is.

SURVEILLANCE AND PRIVACY IN THE PRESENT

It seems that the federal government doesn't want people to be able to keep anything secret from it. One proposed bill—S266, the so-called "counterterrorism" bill introduced by Senators Joseph R. Biden, Jr., (Democarat-Del.) and Dennis DeConcini (Democrat-Ariz.)—would have forced manufacturers of hardware and software that can encrypt data to provide the government with a secret key to break the code. It did not become law . . . this time.

But people like Biden and DeConcini never give up. They'll be back.

RSA Data Security, Inc., has an encryption program that the computer industry wants to use as a standard, but the National Security Agency (NSA) is trying to prevent it because the program is too secure. Even the NSA cannot break it.

The founding fathers could not have conceived of computers in the eighteenth century. If they had, they probably would have mentioned them in the Fourth Amendment, along with personal effects.

It is well known that cellular phones ("the party line of the 1990s") can be easily monitored. There is an effective method of encrypting cellular phone traffic that has already been installed by GTE Mobilnet. This would provide the privacy that vendors promised when the cellular net was new. Apparently the government can use the new method, but as of this writing, it is not available to the general public. The key contained in a signal that goes out on the cellular data channels changes frequently and has already been given to the government, I've been told.

Motorola makes a land-line phone-scrambling system called SVX that is very secure, which the government uses. Try to buy one. Motorola also makes a chip called the Vulcan, built into some of its Saber brand two-way radios, that encrypts transmissions with the DES. The FBI and other federal agencies use these radios, but Motorola does not sell them to the public.

New laws regulate the use of scanners. Florida,

Michigan, and New Jersey have outlawed the use of them in motor vehicles, and more states are likely to follow. Federal intelligence agencies, I have been told, collect names of the purchasers of scanners. Some local police also keep records of people who own them, and bills have been introduced in the U.S. House of Representatives that would require registration of scanners, two-way radios, and possibly even pagers.

Telephone companies keep a computer record of every call made on their systems—not just long distance, every call—which is available to law-enforcement personnel.

When a woman who lived in California's Silicon Valley area disappeared and wasn't heard from for several days, her family called the police. In the investigation, the police learned that the woman had called home and talked to one of her children just after she left. She said she was calling from a pay phone at a nearby convenience store.

The police were able to access the telco records and obtain the number from which the call had actually been placed. It seems that she had set up temporary housekeeping with a bus driver in a nearby city.

The van Eck method of computer snooping, described in Part V, is probably used by the government to eavesdrop on people's personal and business computers, as there is apparently no law against this.

Wang Laboratories was preparing a demonstration on TEMPEST, a method of protecting computers from van Eck, but, allegedly, the feds moved, classified the technology, and convinced Wang to cancel its seminar after threatening to make arrests.

Apparently the federal government doesn't want people to know how to protect *their* computer systems from surveillance, even though it can buy a TEMPEST secure system from Wang to protect its systems. National security?

The trend is clear. Sooner or later Omnibus will be amended, or new laws will be enacted, to further weaken the Fourth Amendment and broaden the power of the government to use surveillance against the people it is supposed to serve.

Why is this happening? One argument is that this oversight power is needed not because the feds are the bad guys, but because they are fighting a losing battle against crime, much of it drug-related. Maybe if we didn't have such a serious drug problem in America, we would all have greater freedom and personal privacy.

On the other hand, maybe the present administration wants a police state. Sometimes it seems that way. When you have a spy for president . . .

There is little we can do to change this, but for now, we can keep them out of our living rooms.

PART I
INSIDE DEVICES

MICROPHONES

The simplest type of bug (generic term used here for any kind of listening device) is an ordinary microphone. It can be hidden anywhere in the area under surveillance with a wire leading to the listening post, which might be an adjoining apartment, in the backyard behind the rhododendron bushes, across a fence, or just about anywhere.

The listener may have a tape recorder or just a small battery-powered amplifier and earphones. The inside wires can be hidden under the edge of carpeting or inside the cracks between a wall and door frame, and the microphone can be as small as a pencil eraser.

A microphone can be used from an apartment or office next to the target, with a small plastic tube inside a wall socket to feed the sound into it. The area inside the walls in which the wiring is installed is usually common to the rooms on both sides in apartment and office buildings. Darken the room, remove the plastic plate from a wall plug, and look in. You might see light coming through the small openings. If light can get out, sound can get out.

A carbon microphone can sometimes be hidden behind the plastic plate that phone wires come through and then be connected to the two unused (black and yellow) wires that are in the phone cable. The listener can be found by following the cable. Listeners can connect these wires to the two unused wires of their own phone cable at the telephone company "66" block at which all the lines enter the building, and they can listen in the comfort of their own apartment. This is called a "bridging tap."

Most, but not all, microphones can be located and made useless with ultrasonic sound (USS) generators.

There are various types of microphone elements. The condenser or "electret" can be very small: 3/8-inch diameter and 1/8-inch thick. The electret requires a small battery, but it can be at the other end of the wire. This is the type that is built into some tape recorders.

The carbon microphone is the type used in telephones. If you have a phone with screw-off caps, take off a cap and take a look. These microphones usually are much larger than the other types and harder to hide, but they can be as small as a quarter.

The carbon microphone requires a DC power source, which is why there is DC voltage on the phone line. Inside are a bunch of small carbon granules. A voice entering the lines changes the resistance of the granules, and these variations are received by another phone as sound. Since it is a DC device, it doesn't pick up humming and interference so it doesn't require expensive shielded cable.

Dynamic and magnetic microphones are the smallest, as tiny as 1/4-inch square and 1/8-inch thick, and do not require a power source. These and the Electret are AC devices and usually need shielded cable, an inside wire that has a grounded braided copper covering. Long unshielded wires attached to them act as antennas and pick up noise, usually the 60-cycle hum from power lines and appliances that interferes with the sound. Also, there is audio equipment to prevent this problem so these microphones will work on ordinary phone-line type (unshielded) wires.

Another problem with microphones is that the sound they receive can fade as the distance between them and the people being listened to increases. The sound can also become distorted in a room with poor acoustics. A microphone preamplifier will improve the quality of the sound, as will equalizers and certain types of filters. Viking International has some good audio gear that will correct this problem, including the model 12DB preamplifier.

Contact Microphones

A common microphone is the contact type, sometimes called an electronic stethoscope. This is the device that magazine ads claim can "hear through walls," and it can do just that with varying degrees of success, depending on the quality of the device, the thickness and composition of the walls, and the background noise.

Try placing the open end of an ordinary drinking glass against the wall of the room you are in, and press your ear tightly against the bottom to see what you can hear in the next room. A contact microphone will hear much more, and the better ones will have equalizers or band pass filters to help eliminate unwanted sounds and vibrations.

The famous "spike microphone" is a contact microphone mounted on the end of a nail or spike that is first driven into a wall so that the tip is touching the inside of the wall of the room to be listened in on.

There is no way to detect a contact microphone, but anything that causes the wall to vibrate slightly will make it difficult if not impossible for anyone to hear your conversations. A four-dollar transistor radio will do the job just fine. Remove the plastic case and tape it to the wall, near the center, with the speaker pressed directly to the surface. Cover it with anything handy to deaden the sound so it isn't a distraction and hang a picture over it. Tuned to a twenty-four-hour news station, it will be most discouraging to eavesdroppers, though they will be well-informed on current events and weather forecasts.

A microphone might be used instead of an RF transmitter for long-term surveillance in a place in which it would be difficult to use the 120-volt lighting circuit for power or a bug with large and long-lasting batteries would be difficult to hide. A carbon microphone is about a dollar at surplus stores or may be removed from an old phone for free.

The Tube

Many years ago, before telephones and electronic intercoms were invented, communicating aboard a ship was done through metal speaking tubes. The helmsman had a metal cone that he yelled into to talk to the engine-room crew, who answered in the same way.

Private homes and most small apartment buildings are wired with Romex heavy-plastic insulated cable that carries electricity to wall plugs and switches from the service or circuit breaker box. Commercial buildings and large office and apartment buildings are wired with "speaking tubes." The electrical conduit (electrical metallic tubing, or EMT) that contains the power lines will carry sound just like the speaking tubes aboard yesterday's ships.

In a large building, these tubes make up a complex maze that go up and down inside walls, elevator shafts, and air-vent shafts, and across ceilings.

The steel boxes in which two conduits join or branch off are called handi-boxes, and the ones that hold switches and wall plugs are called switch boxes. A microphone can be hidden inside one of these boxes or in the main service panel in the basement maintenance area, and it will pick up the sound that gets into the tubes. How well this works—how much can be heard and how clear it will be—depends on a number of things.

In a smaller building with fewer "conversations" in the tube and with the microphone in a box close to the target, it works quite well. If placed in the main panel in a large building, it becomes something of a party line, with dozens of people talking at the same time. Audio filtering equipment will improve the sound.

With good equipment—a high gain amplifier with filtering equipment—reception can be improved considerably.

There aren't any types of electronic equipment that will detect a microphone inside a handi-box, but defeating this method of listening is simple: fill all of the switch boxes with something that blocks the sound.

Liquid Seal-Flex will do, as will Insta-Foam aerosol packing foam. Do not use anything that absorbs moisture, such as cloth or paper, because it is a potential fire hazard. Different cities have different codes concerning this, and there is also the

National Electric Code (NEC) to be considered. Call the fire marshall or a commercial electrician for precise regulations in your area.

THE RADIO SPECTRUM

A word of explanation about frequency bands is in order before we get into RF (radio frequency) transmitters. Sound (audio), RF (radio and TV waves), light, etc., are all part of the electromagnetic spectrum, and they all vibrate at various rates or frequencies in cycles per second or hertz, the term most people use. I prefer cycles.

The audio spectrum begins with infrasonic sound, from 1 to 20 cycles per second, and then audible sound, from about 20 to 20,000 cycles per second. Above sound is ultrasonic sound, and then radio frequency (RF) or radio waves begin.

The area within the electromagnetic spectrum in which radio waves operate is called the radio spectrum. The lowest RF area starts at about 6,000 cycles. This overlaps with the audio portion, but it is still considered part of the radio spectrum, which is divided into the following groups:

- VLF—Very low frequency, from 6,000 cycles or 6 kilocycles (kc.) to 30 kc. Used mainly for marine navigation and communication.
- LF—Low frequency, from 30,000 cycles or 30 kc. to 300,000 cycles or 300 kc. per second. Also used mainly by the maritime services.
- MF—Medium frequency, from 300 kc. to 3,000 kc. or 3 megacycles or millioncycles (mc.). AM broadcasting is in this band.
- HF—High frequency, from 3 to 30 mc. It is used for all types of communications, including international shortwave broadcasting, ham radio, citizens band, law enforcement, etc.
- VHF—Very high frequency, from 30 to 300 mc. Almost all bugs transmit in this area. A few rare exceptions are microwave and the MF ones mentioned in this chapter.
- UHF—Ultrahigh frequency, from 300 to 3,000 mc. or 3 gigacycles or billioncycles (gc.). UHF television and public-service stations—police and other local government agencies that use repeaters operate from this range.
- SHF—Superhigh frequency, from 3 to 30 gc.

This and EHF are the microwave bands, which are used for communications, navigation, space exploration, and satellite transmissions.

- EHF—Extremely high frequency, from 30 to 300 gc. At 300 gc., radio waves end, and infrared light begins. Then there is visible light, ultraviolet light, X rays, gamma rays, and, finally, cosmic rays from outer space.

An interesting poster-size chart, called the United States Frequency Allocations, shows the electromagnectic spectrum in detail and is available from the U.S. Government Printing Office.

RF TRANSMITTERS

Anything that transmits can be used as a bug. This will be discussed in detail a little later, but transmitters all have a few things in common: they require a microphone, an antenna, and a power source that is usually a battery. If the transmitter is hidden inside a lamp, clock, or wall plug, it can use the power lines to operate.

Remote Control

The remote-control bug is essentially the same as any other bug. It can be large or small and can be turned on or off from a remote location with a device no more complicated than a garage-door opener.

The listener can activate the remote, and if he doesn't hear anything, he can shut it off and try later. This makes the device more difficult to find and conserves the battery. One of these placed inside a large book with several D-cell batteries can last for months.

Repeater Transmitters

One of the more sophisticated types of bugs is the repeater, which uses the same principle as commercial two-way radios used by taxi companies, police agencies, etc. The mobile units send out a signal that is received by the repeater unit located on top of a mountain or other high place and is rebroadcast from this higher location at a higher power level, thus greatly increasing the range.

For example, using a portable (hand-held) radio in Santa Cruz, California, I have talked through a repeater to someone on Nob Hill in San Francisco, fifty-eight miles away.

When a repeater system is used for surveillance, a very small RF transmitter is hidden somewhere inside the area to be bugged. The small size makes it easier to hide and harder to find. The repeater used to relay its signal to the listening post can be placed in an adjoining office, inside a wall, on the roof, or on the outside of the building.

I once knew a man who managed a commercial window-washing company, who told about some of the "temporary help" occasionally provided by the owner of the company. The manager related that these people didn't know a damn thing about cleaning windows—their hands were too clean for them to be working people—and he was told that sometimes they would go up by themselves, and he was to leave them alone.

A repeater transmitter is usually hidden in a light fixture or sign where it can be connected to the power lines. Its higher output often requires more power than a battery can provide. For example, a repeater about the size of a videocassette can have a power output of as much as 30 watts, and fitted with a directional antenna, it can transmit as many miles. That kind of power would drain a car battery overnight.

A repeater system is often used in a situation in which a listening post can't be set up close to the target, such as in a rural area or an upper-middle-class neighborhood where it is not easy to rent an office or apartment and a suspicious van or other vehicle would likely be noticed and reported.

A repeater is not the easiest surveillance system to set up, and it isn't likely to be used for short-term surveillance. Access can be a problem, and it is expensive and not usually retrieved.

One of the rules in surveillance is: "If you find it, you own it." Surveillance has to be cost-effective like anything else—except perhaps for the writing of books about surveillance.

Burst Transmitter

The burst transmitter is a special (and expensive) RF device. Instead of sending a continuous signal, it stores what it hears and periodically transmits it in a fraction-of-a-second burst. This technique is used in satellite transmissions. Since it transmits for such a short period of time, it is difficult to home in on it with bug detectors.

The sound in the target area is picked up by a microphone and then converted into digital form in the same way it is described in Part II on secure phone communications.

Once in digital form, the information is stored in memory chips, the same way in which data are stored in computer memory, and when the memory is full, it is dumped to the transmitter and goes out in a burst.

Using the newer (and smaller) surface-mount chips, the burst transmitter and the batteries are about the size of two 35mm film boxes, depending on how much memory the transmitter has and how well it was designed. At this size, it can store about 10 to 15 minutes of sound.

The burst transmitter is too expensive to be used for short-term surveillance, and the size of it and its batteries (probably four penlight or larger cells) makes it harder to hide. Since it is not feasible in most circumstances for a spy to penetrate the target regularly to replace batteries, the burst transmitter is most likely inside something that plugs into the lighting circuit.

The burst transmitter is one of the most difficult bugs to detect. It can use a carbon microphone, which ultrasonic sound devices will not locate, and if it is well shielded, the nonlinear junction device (NLJD, described later) will not detect it. A piece of equipment that is effective in finding the burst transmitter is the countersurveillance monitor model CPM-700 made by REI. This device covers 50 kc. to 3 gc. and has a "time check" feature that records the time that a signal is received. I haven't used this monitor, but intelligence professionals who use it whenever they sweep for bugs swear by it. A careful physical search can also detect the present generation of burst transmitters.

The burst transmitter is not something that the average electronic technician can build easily—at least not in a small space. It requires extensive design and layout work and several circuit boards stacked atop one another. All things considered, it is very expensive to make. If one were to hire an electrical engineer to build one, it would cost several thousand dollars for the prototype.

Microwave Transmitter

A microwave bug is like other RF-type

mitters except that it transmits on microwave frequencies. One microwave engineer told me that he has seen transmitters that are one-fourth the size of a cigarette package, have an output of 100 milliwatts, and work in the 10 to 11 gc. range. Under the right conditions, 100 mw. can have a range of several blocks. I have never seen one of these. At this frequency range only a microwave receiver or a spectrum analyzer can detect the RF signal.

Microwave bugs are also highly directional. Low frequencies bend and follow the curvature of the Earth, which is called ground wave. Radio stations on low frequencies can be received thousands of miles away. Microwaves are "line of sight" and travel in a straight line, which has some effect on where they can be used.

This and their cost make them rare. Since they are inside devices, the spies who install them aren't likely to get them back. A professional will seldom even try to retrieve bugs—it is too dangerous. The following is one of the few examples of a spy being caught in the act.

We found a transmitter hidden inside a hot-air register while sweeping the area with a bug detector. We decided to try to draw out the person who had hidden it, so we hid a small video camera inside the room, and then disabled the bug. The next evening the camera recorded a woman opening the register to fix it. She was a temporary employee provided by an agency.

Microwave surveillance is generally an outside method of gathering information.

Low Frequency

One of the countersurveillance experts I interviewed told me that he had never encountered a bug that operated in the LF-MF band. These transmitters are rare, but they have been used. This makes the LF band a good place for a bug to transmit because no one expects to find it there, and many bug detectors will not tune this low-frequency area.

One reason that bugs traditionally have not been used on LF is that it is an AM band. Almost all the radios that operate there—short-wave amateur radio, international broadcasting, and others—are AM. AM is much more vulnerable to static and other interfer-

ence. Ever notice on your car radio that on AM you hear static and whining from nearby cars, whistling, and other noises that you do not hear on FM?

An FM bug can be built to work on high frequency (HF), but back in the early days of surveillance transmitters, most receivers would not receive FM on low frequency. So FM bugs were used on the higher band, VHF, which is almost exclusively FM, and the tradition continues.

The spectrum analyzer will find an LF bug, and there are a number of receivers that cover LF and will receive both AM and FM.

The AR-3000 scanner covers LF (and everything else). It costs about $1,000 and can be interfaced to a computer by using an optional software package. This is a good scanner, but it is sometimes in short supply because the manufacturer doesn't mass produce them. Try Scanners Unlimited in San Carlos, California, or EEB in the Washington, D.C., area.

The ICOM R-71A communications receiver tunes 100 kc. to 30 mc. and is an excellent radio. It costs about $850.

The top of the line is the ICOM R9000, which receives 100 kc. to 2 gc. in all modes (including TV) and has a built-in computer, including data/video display screen. It sells for about $4,500.

Other receivers that cover LF are by Kenwood, Yaesu, and Japan Radio, all of which are comparable. I prefer ICOM, but they are all good radios.

I know for a fact that LF bugs have been used. If you call in a team of debuggers, ask them to check for them. Or buy a receiver and check yourself, but be warned, shortwave radio listening is a fascinating and addicting hobby.

INFRARED TRANSMITTERS

Infrared bugs pick up and amplify sound just like RF bugs, but they transmit on a beam of invisible light. The principle is similar to the remote-control device for a TV set.

It is simple to build an infrared transmitter; in fact, it is one of the devices that first-year electronics students can choose as a lab exercise. Two small chips and a dozen other small components are all that you need for a finished product that is about one-inch square and that has an effective range of several hundred feet or more, depending on how it is made.

The receiver is also simple: a small filter passes through the IR light, which strikes a photocell. The variations of the light cause the photocell to generate a voltage with the same variations, which feed into a small amplifier and come out as sound.

The advantage of such a device is that it won't be found by most conventional RF bug detectors, but Capri has an optional probe that will "see" infrared light.

Its disadvantages are twofold: it has to be placed so that the beam of light is pointed out a window, and the batteries used to power it are much larger than the device itself. It normally uses TTL circuits that operate on 5 volts so it most often will use four penlight cells. Some types use CMOS, which can use a standard 9-volt battery, but this makes it easier to find during the physical search. Depending on how it is designed, the batteries may last a few days or a couple of weeks, but not months or years, thus limiting the time frame of the surveillance.

VISIBLE-LIGHT TRANSMITTERS

You are sitting in your favorite chair in the living room of your home, talking to your spouse about personal matters that you would never discuss with anyone else. Several blocks down the street, an eavesdropper has a telescope pointed at your picture window and is hearing, and tape-recording, every word you say.

This ingenious and insidious technique for eavesdropping is the most unsuspected and difficult-to-find listening device of all. It is called the light modulator.

The principle is the same as that of the IR device except that the signal is transmitted by an ordinary light bulb. The one in the table lamp beside your easy chair will do nicely. A microphone inside the lamp picks up and amplifies the sound in the room and then channels it into a circuit that causes the voltage going to the lamp to vary according to the sound from the audio amplifier. The voltage is varied only about 10 percent, so the changes in brightness are so slight you would never notice it.

The listening post can be anywhere from which the light can be seen, and with a telescope, that can be a considerable distance. Even if the curtains are closed, it will still work if enough light shows

through: it is the variations in the light and not the intensity that sends the intelligence.

How well it works depends on the sensitivity of the receiver and the quality of the audio equipment used. Because there is no RF signal, bug detectors and the spectrum analyzer will miss it. By using a carbon microphone and shielding the light modulator, the operator can hide it from conventional debugging equipment.

It costs less than $50 to build a light modulator, but getting it into your target's lamp can be difficult. Installing it requires taking the lamp apart and doing some wiring that takes perhaps ten to twenty minutes. The modulating device can also be placed inside the wall socket into which the lamp is plugged.

A visible-light transmitter can be detected in at least four ways. First, the same probe for the TD-53 bug detector that detects IR will also see the variations in light.

Second, use a voltmeter to measure the voltage from the bulb socket (not the outlet) while there is some sound in the room. It should be a steady 110 to 120 volts and not vary at all. If the needle swings back and forth, you have just found a bug. Now measure the voltage from the plug to see if it is there or in the lamp.

Third, a good photographer's "spot" light meter will show any flickering.

Fourth, a physical search will uncover the device. Take the lamp apart. The lamp cord should go directly to the switch and then the socket. There should not be any kind of electrical device, printed circuit board, microphone, small wires, etc., in the lamp. Then look inside the switchbox (the "universal hiding place") for the types of extraneous devices, wires, etc.

The visible-light transmitter is a clever device. Beware of peddlers crying, "New lamps for old."

WIRELESS INTERCOMS

Sometimes called subcarrier transceivers, wireless intercoms are like conventional intercoms, except that the signals are sent through power lines. Some wireless baby monitors use this technique.

The range of subcarrier devices is limited to those power lines that are from the same line transformer, the kind you see on some telephone poles. They step from 12,000-21,000 volts down to 120 volts used in lighting circuits. Because of the characteristics of these transformers, the signals can't get through them and into the next transformer and the lighting circuits it feeds.

One such transformer can supply approximately twenty single-family houses, one hundred apartments, or a medium-size office building—which tells you approximately from how far away it is effective.

The signal from a subcarrier device can be detected by a device made for this purpose, such as the one available from Capri Electronics. The microphone can usually be detected with ultrasonic sound.

If you have one of these in your home, keep in mind that others can listen in on it from other apartments or down the street . . .

• • •

With inside devices, there are trade-offs. A wireless microphone can be inexpensive, but it has a short range and battery life. The burst transmitter is harder to find with surveillance gear, but it is larger and more expensive. A repeater has almost unlimited range, but it is expensive and can be difficult to install. You must consider all these things before deciding upon the type of bug to use. You will understand this better after reading the section on physical searches for surveillance devices in Part III.

PART II
TELEPHONE SURVEILLANCE

AN OVERVIEW

Never assume that your telephone conversations are secure. Even if you aren't being bugged, what about the person on the other end of the line?

There are ten basic methods of intercepting phone conversations:

1. Direct listening wiretaps
2. Remote listening wiretaps
3. Down-line taps
4. SO and REMOBS
5. Cordless phone monitoring
6. Cellular phone monitoring
7. Answering machine hacking
8. Voice mail hacking
9. Microwave and satellite interception
10. Phone tricks

DIRECT LISTENING WIRE TAPS

The first method is just like the hidden microphone in the preceding section, except that the wires are connected to a phone line and strung to the listening post, or existing wires are used.

At the listening post, the wiretapper might use a lineman's test set, an ordinary telephone, or a "listen down the line" amplifier, but most likely he will use a modified tape recorder. Experienced spies always tape-record what they hear.

The recorder will probably have a "drop-out" relay that interfaces it to the phone line. This device turns the recorder on when the phone is being used

and turns it off again when the phone is hung up. Drop-out relays are available from many places, such as Sherwood Communications.

In a private home, the listening post can be in the backyard, or the wire can lead across a fence to a neighbor's yard (or house). It can also be inside the house, using the tape recorder and drop-out relay, as was done in one case with which I am familiar.

The whole family was a bunch of thieves. They burglarized people's homes, stole anything they could from where they worked—even if they had no use for it—and at school Steve took everything he could get his hands on. Steve asked another student to share a house with him, his wife, and brothers. The student agreed, and they rented a large home near the campus. After a while, he realized what Steve and his family were really like and became concerned about his computer and electronic equipment.

After thinking about it for a long time, he decided to bug them and installed a Marantz tape recorder and a drop-out relay on the phone line they shared.

It wasn't long before he found out that Steve and one of his brothers were planning to fake a burglary just after graduation and steal all his expensive equipment and take it with them in a rented moving truck when they moved back to their family home in Virginia.

The roommate and a friend decided to set up the thieves. They hid in the friend's van in front of the house and photographed them in the act of loading the stuff into the rented truck. Caught in the act, they were given a choice: load up their belongings, leave town and don't come back, or be arrested. They headed south.

The direct method is the same in private homes and office or apartment buildings, but the wiretaps are sometimes wired in different ways.

Each unit may have its own small four-wire cable, like those used in private homes, or there may be a larger cable with wires for twenty-five, fifty, or one hundred phones that loops through the building from the main phone line connection panel, sometimes called a "sixty-six block."

In older buildings, this block may be on the basement wall where anyone can access it. Newer buildings usually have the phone wiring in a secured area called a distribution closet. At each unit, the small four-wire cable branches off from the large one, enters through a small hole drilled in the wall, and is connected to the plastic modular jack, or to an opening in the wall covered with a plastic plate (the same size as a wall plug or light switch) that has the modular jack built into it.

If multiline cable is used, then anyone can tap into any of the lines inside it. To select a particular line, the tapper has to know which it is by the colors of the wires inside the cable (more on this in Part III).

REMOTE LISTENING WIRETAPS: TYPES OF RF PHONE BUGS

An RF phone bug is a transmitter, the same as in the preceding example except that it is connected to the telephone line instead of a microphone. Obviously, it will not pick up the sounds inside the room where it is placed, only what is spoken over the telephone.

There are several ways to use an RF phone bug. It may be direct or inductive. A direct tap is wired to the phone line and may be series or parallel. The series usually draws its power from the phone line, and the parallel usually has a battery to provide power.

An inductive tap uses a coil of wire placed close to a phone or the phone line and picks up the conversation from the electromagnetic field that radiates from the phone or the line. And again, as with direct listen, the wiretapper has to know which line to tap.

If the target is a private home, then it's obvious which pair to use, but as before, the spies have to get into the house, backyard, or basement to tap the line.

In old apartment buildings, especially big houses that have been converted into apartments, the phone wires are strung all over the basement area. New wires, old wires, and ancient wires are everywhere. This is a wiretapper's dream. Access is usually easy, the phone lines are often tagged with the apartment number, and the places in which to tap the line are almost unlimited. There is plenty of space for a large (and long-lasting) battery, and often the doorbell wires are right beside the phone wires, which is like manna from heaven: the listener taps the doorbell line, changes it to DC, and uses it to power the bug.

A bug in such a place can accommodate a very powerful transmitter, and there is plenty of space for a long antenna so the range is virtually unlimited —literally miles.

Louis, an easygoing type of guy, was well-liked by everyone, including the employees at the furniture store he owned. Louis had been dating a girl named Cindy for several months, and although he hadn't mentioned it to her yet, he was thinking they might eventually get married. One evening he was at a cocktail lounge, wishing he were with Cindy, who had told him she would be out of town for a few days visiting her family. After a while, Louis left the bar, and as he was getting into his car, he saw Cindy with another man going in.

Hurt and shaken, Louis sat there for a while, thinking, and then went home. Cindy had told Louis that he was the only man she was seeing, and he was upset by her lying as well as the fact that he had extended her more than three thousand dollars in credit for new furniture.

The next day when he confronted her, she tried to lie her way out of it by saying he was mistaken, that she hadn't been at the bar. She finally broke down and admitted that she had, but she told him it was "too bad because there isn't anything you can do about it." When he asked if she was going to pay for the furniture, she replied, "You gave it to me, and I don't owe you anything."

Louis felt sick inside. He was hurt and angry, and

he decided to get even. He had some knowledge of electronics from his days in the navy, so he built a large transmitter from a radio using plans obtained from an old issue of Popular Electronics. *He installed the transmitter in the basement of her apartment building.*

For three weeks people in the neighborhood of the medium-size city in Michigan listened to her lie to and use half a dozen men, telling each that he was the only one in her life, and then bragging to her girlfriends about all the money and gifts she had conned from them.

When someone finally told her about what was happening, she freaked out and decided (for real) to go and stay with her family. A neighbor saw her load some things into a station wagon, and she never came back to the old neighborhood. Louis got his furniture back, but the hurt and bitterness stayed with him a long time.

We think Cindy deserved what she got, and we sympathize with Louis, but this still does not justify what he did. He was not defending himself; he was getting even. And what about the right to privacy of the many people to whom Cindy talked?

Line-Powered Remote Wiretaps

As the name implies, such phone bugs receive power from the voltage on the phone lines, which typically is 48 volts. The power of this type is low compared to other types, because of the load it places on the line. If the load is too great, the bug will be detected automatically by the telco maintenance equipment.

Line-powered bugs are in all other respects the same as other types of RF phone bugs: they are attached to the line, and they transmit what is being said on the line to a nearby receiver.

Drop-In Remote Wiretaps

The drop-in is an ordinary carbon telephone microphone that has a small line-powered bug built into it. Because it uses a small line-powered bug, the drop-in has a limited range, approximately one hundred feet.

It was invented back in the 1960s when almost all telephones were built by Western Electric and used the same type of mouthpiece. In just a few

seconds, the Bakelite cap could be unscrewed and the replacement dropped in, hence the name.

The handset (receiver) of many of today's phones are molded in two parts and screwed together, but if you have a phone with the screw-off caps and you suspect such a device, you can just replace the microphone or the whole phone. Since the drop-in is line-powered, it will not work once it is removed or the phone is disconnected from the line.

Series and Parallel

These two are also two variations of the basic RF phone bug. The bug has two wires coming out of it. With the parallel bug, the two wires are just spliced across the two phone line wires. With a series bug, one of the phone wires is cut, and the two open ends go to the bug's two wires. A parallel bug is usually battery-powered, and the series device is usually line-powered—usually, but not always.

There is a difference in how they affect the line, which will be described in the section in Part III on finding phone bugs.

The Infinity Transmitter

The infinity transmitter is not really a transmitter like the RF devices described above. It is a remote-controlled device used to listen in on the room where the target phone is located.

The infinity device is wired inside the target phone (or some versions have a built-in microphone and are hidden somewhere else in the area) from which it can be connected to the phone line and

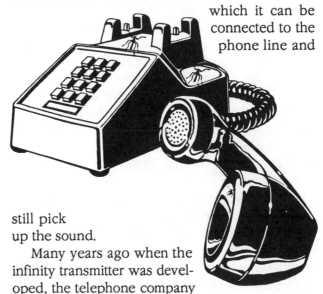

still pick up the sound.

Many years ago when the infinity transmitter was developed, the telephone company used mechanical stepping switches or relays (crossbars) to connect one line to another. If you called a number, the switches or relays would make an electrical connection between your line and the one you called as soon as you dialed the last number.

Once the connection was made, the called phone was turned on, and the mouthpiece or built-in microphone was hot. This is called a hook switch bypass. The listener would then send a tone down the line that would stop the phone from ringing. This was originally done with a harmonica, and the device was called a harmonica bug.

The Electronic Switching System (ESS) now used by the telco will not connect the two lines together until the called line answers, so infinity transmitters that worked with the crossbar switching systems won't work with the ESS. Other types will.

The new types intercept and store the voltage that causes a phone to ring for a fraction of a second and then place a resistance across the line that simulates its answering.

In this short period of time, it listens for its activation tone, like the harmonica note used with the old type. If it hears this tone, the phone is answered, and the microphone becomes hot. If not, it releases the stored ring voltage, and the phone rings as usual. The bypass can be deactivated by sending another tone, and the phone will then function normally.

Infinity transmitters that work on the ESS systems are hard to come by; they are not likely to be found in "spy shops" or mail-order catalogs.

Another device that is similar to the infinity transmitter is advertised as a "burglar alarm" or "telemonitor." If placed on a phone line, it will "answer" the line and activate its self-contained microphone, but it will not prevent the phones on that line from ringing. If the listener were to disable the ringers in the phones on the target line, this device would then work as an infinity transmitter and prevent the phones from ringing, but before long someone would start to wonder why no one was calling him or her anymore.

These devices sell for $150 to $200, which is too much for most people to spend on something that isn't likely to work for more than a day or so.

Telemonitors are intended to be used with a dedicated line that has no phones on it. An example of the telemonitor is the Panasonic KX-T2432 Auto-Logic remote-controlled answering machine, which has a function called "answer back."

To use it, you call from any phone, and when it answers, punch in a code number from the Touchtone pad and the built-in microphone will turn on, allowing you to hear what is being said in the room where the phone is placed. It stays on for only thirty seconds, but it demonstrates how telemonitors work.

Telemonitors are legal if not used to listen to someone without his or her knowledge and are available from Sherwood.

Subcarrier Extensions

A subcarrier extension system couples a phone line to the AC power line so that an extension phone can be plugged into any AC wall outlet using a small adapter. The principle is the same as wireless intercoms and baby monitors.

Some companies that sell these systems imply that the signal can't be received outside your own home. This is untrue, as you learned in the section on wireless intercoms. If you have such a system, keep this in mind, or better yet, take it back to the place you bought it from and demand your money back. Tell the clerk that you were a victim of false advertising.

A subcarrier extension system can be used for surveillance by hiding it somewhere in the target area from which both power and phone lines can be accessed—in the basement of an apartment building or in your garage if you have an extension phone there.

Like wireless intercoms, the CD-01 subcarrier detector from Capri Electronics will find a subcarrier extension.

DOWN-LINE TAPS

A down-line tap is generally defined as any tap that is outside the area over which one has control or to which one has access to—one that is off the premises. This could be outside of a house or office building or anywhere from the telephone pole in an alley to inside the telco's underground junction points. A down-line tap can be either direct or remote. Down-line taps are uncommon for a number of reasons, which are explained in Part III on searching phone lines.

REMOBS EAVESDROPPING

REMOBS stands for Remote Observance. REMOBS is a way to listen in on a phone line from another (remote) phone line. If your phone were tapped under a court order, the telco could then program its computer to tie it to a second (REMOBS) line, which goes directly to the agency that obtained the order.

At the offices of that agency, the listeners would set up their tape recorders and whatever else they do in these situations. They probably have dedicated lines for this purpose. Of course, I do not know that they do, but since it is a legal tap, it is doubtful that two agents and three tape recorders would take up residence in a cramped distribution closet. (This makes it hard to send out for a pizza.) This is one example of REMOBS.

The following is the true account of something that happened that leads me to think that there is another way to use REMOBS.

About two years ago, when I first heard of remote observance, I tried to learn more about it. All I knew at the time, actually what I had heard rather than knew, was what I stated above: that it is a way to tap one phone from another.

I started by calling Pacific Bell. Everyone I talked to said he never heard of it. I expected that. I wandered around looking for telco trucks and pestered some of the workers with questions, but everyone said he didn't know what it was. Some of them were lying—I can't prove it, but one can sometimes tell when someone is being untruthful.

Then I left messages on a number of computer bulletin boards asking anyone who knew anything about REMOBS to call; the message also stated that there were two lines to use for a demonstration. I gave the number of line one, but not line two, which was billed to the first. Both numbers were unlisted and unpublished.

A few weeks later I received a call from someone who did not give a name. He said he could demonstrate REMOBS. He asked me to make a call on the second line. Since I didn't want to make anyone else a party to this, I called a number that I figured would put me on hold for a while. I called Pacific Bell.

A few seconds after the call was answered and the synthesized voice was saying something about the high volume of calls, the caller came in on line two, while he was still on line one, and there was no "click." I started to ask how he did it, but he cut me off and offered a second demonstration. I was told to call a bulletin board system (BBS).

The line went silent, but the dial tone did not come back on. I pushed the hook switch and got the dial tone back, hung up, and called a computer BBS, and about a minute after I logged on, the anonymous caller—still on line one—started reading back everything I was typing on the computer as I typed it. I tried to get him to explain, but he said he had to go. I never heard from him again.

Have you ever picked up your phone to make a call and found that someone else was on the line trying to make a call? Have you ever called a number that wouldn't ring, and then heard people talking in the background?

Some observations:

- I had a voltmeter on both lines to monitor the line voltage. It is set by the telco at 48 volts, and while it varies depending on a number of things, it should be between 46 and 52. When the phone is "off hook," it drops to about 12 volts, and if a second phone is picked up, it drops a little lower. When the caller came in on line two, it dropped from 12 to 9 volts.

- I didn't tell the anonymous caller the number of the second line. In the first demo, I didn't tell him whom I was calling from line two. In the second demo, I didn't tell him the number or the name of the computer BBS I called. The system has only one incoming line.

- There are ways of getting unlisted numbers. That part was no surprise, but somehow he tapped into line two both by voice and computer.

- Some people have suggested that this was done by a telco employee who was in the switching office (SO) at the time. That is one possibility.

- A countersurveillance expert I discussed this with suggested that he tapped the line into the apartment building. That's the first thing I checked. The SPSP boxes where our lines came in were secured in such a way that I would know if they had been opened. There is no other place they could have been tapped without removing the insulation from and splicing a wire to the line. This had not been done.

Pacific Bell will deny that what I have described is possible, but I am not convinced. Every phone line in the telco system goes into, and is controlled by, its mainframe computer system, which is, has to be, capable of connecting any line to any other line. With the right access codes, passwords, and the like, it seems logical that someone could use REMOBS.

All I know is what happened.

CORDLESS TELEPHONES

Cordless telephones operate under provisions of the FCC "low power" laws, which limit them to 100 milliwatts (1/10 watt) power. They are advertised as having a range of 100 feet, 200 feet, etc. This is true with the antennas that the base and handset use and the sensitivity of the receivers.

However, a good scanner with an antenna on top of a house or building can pick up cordless phones much further away. Depending on terrain and obstructions, range can be from several blocks to more than a mile.

Practically every scanner made, from the cheapest ten-channel available for $50 in pawn shops to the top-of-the-line models like the AR-3000, receives cordless phone frequencies. Cordless phones have ten channels with separate frequencies for base and handset. These frequencies for base and handset respectively are:

CHANNEL 01	46.610	49.670
CHANNEL 02	46.630	49.845
CHANNEL 03	46.670	49.860
CHANNEL 04	46.710	49.770
CHANNEL 05	46.730	49.875
CHANNEL 06	46.770	49.830
CHANNEL 07	46.830	49.890
CHANNEL 08	46.870	49.930
CHANNEL 09	46.930	49.990
CHANNEL 10	46.970	49.970

Some older cordless phones operate on other frequencies. They are listed in Appendix D.

Hundreds of thousands of scanners have been sold in the United States, so keep this in mind when you use a cordless phone. Also be suspicious if some mail-order company sends you one as a "marketing test" or whatever. This has been done . . .

CELLULAR TELEPHONES

In the section on surveillance law, I mentioned that there is a law that allows people to listen to some types of radio-telephone conversations but not others. This law is the Electronic Communications Privacy Act (ECPA), which prohibits monitoring both cordless and cellular phones. Part of this law has been reversed by the U.S. Supreme Court, which, as I understand it, states that "no reasonable expectation of privacy" exists on cordless phone frequencies, so apparently they can be monitored legally.

The Omnibus Crime Control and Safe Streets Act of 1968 doesn't seem to cover cordless phones, either, but I don't know for sure. Consult a lawyer rather than take my word for this.

Listening to cellular radio is still against the law (ECPA). Why one is legal and the other is not, I do not understand. They both use a duplex two-way radio, both are connected to phone lines at one end (or both), the frequencies of both are public-domain information, and scanners that can receive both without being modified are on the market. According to the law, a person using a cellular phone has a "reasonable expectation of privacy." In reality, that person does not.

Some salespeople in cellular phone stores will try to convince you otherwise. I went into one store in Chicago, pretending to want to buy a phone, and told a salesperson that I was concerned about people listening in with scanners and asked if this was possible.

"Certainly not," he replied. "By law, scanners aren't allowed to be sold in this country if they can receive 'our' frequencies, and they are kept confidential."

With the righteous indignation of confronted liars, he continued, "Even if someone had these frequencies, he couldn't hear anyone for more than a few seconds because the channels change every few seconds." None of what he said is true.

Whereas cordless phones operate on only one of 10 channels, cellular phones have 820 channels; each of the two vendors uses 410 of them. As the phone moves from one area to another, it changes from one channel to another. This makes it harder to stay with or track any one conversation. It is difficult, but far from impossible. Cellular telephones have greater range, as the antennas are usually on top of towers or tall buildings, and tracking requires only a good scanner with at least 200 memory channels (400 is better), a good outside antenna, and the expertise to program it effectively.

With such a scanner it is possible to track the same conversation throughout most of a large city and some suburban areas, and if the phone stays in one place, the scanner won't change channels. Some conversations have continued for hours without the scanner's ever-changing channels.

It is not possible to just dial up a particular cellular phone with a scanner, but if you know that the caller is in a certain area and recognize the voice, you can find him if he stays on the air for at least five minutes. It is also easy to follow the vehicle as he drives and to stay with the conversation, as described in Appendix F.

To tap into a given phone or to be able to tell whenever that particular phone goes on the air, you need a system access monitor (SAM). A portable SAM that is close to a cellular phone will 1) receive the signals it sends (called Capture Voice Channel Assignment), 2) display on the front panel, and 3) store for later printing all of the information in the phone's NAM (number assignment module), including, among others, the Mobile Identification Number (MIN) and Electronic Serial Number (ESN).

Once you have the numbers, you can scan the

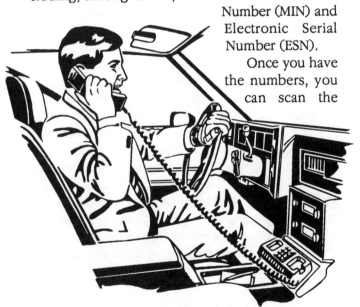

cellular system data channels with the SAM and look for them. You can also monitor the single control channel used for incoming calls and tell when a call is placed to that phone. SAMs sell for $1,200 to $1,400.

With some cellular phones, it is possible to duplicate these numbers and burn them into the NAM chip of another phone. It works on the pirated number just like the real phone.

I have been told that vendors have added some new security methods to prevent this. Check with a local vendor or the manufacturer. Someone could run up a large bill on your account, and you wouldn't know it until the next statement came.

Whenever you use your cellular phone, remember that there is a good chance that someone, somewhere, is listening.

For more information on how the cellular system works, see the article on how cellular radio works in Appendix F.

Some scanners and communications receivers receive the cellular bands without modification, including the ICOM R7000 and R9000 receivers and the AR-1000 and AR-3000 scanners. Others are easily modified. Details on how to do this are in Appendix G.

ANSWERING MACHINES

If I were to call your phone number and get an answering machine that has the remote-control feature, I could listen to, record, and erase your recorded messages if I wanted to.

Using a computer program that generates the pairs of DTMF (Dual Tone, Multifrequency) Touchtone frequencies, I called my machine from my second line, and although it took five attempts, I was able to break into it. Written in BASIC, what this program does is to generate all of the tones sequentially from 000 to 999, which can then be tape-recorded, and used from a pay phone.

"Phreaketh thee never phrom thine own phone phor surely thou wilt be phound and thy computer taken phrom thee."

From the Hacker's Ten Commandments.

Touchtones are actually different pairs of frequencies for each of the twelve keys. In addition to these twelve, there are four other tones that the Touchtone pad can generate: A, B, C, and D in the chart. These are not included in standard telephones but are used by the military Autovon system. They are Flash, Immediate, Priority, and Routine.

These frequencies, in cycles per second, are:

KEY	FREQ1	FREQ2	KEY	FREQ1	FREQ2
1	697	1209	4	770	1209
2	697	1336	5	770	1336
3	697	1477	6	770	1477
A	697	1633	B	770	1633
7	852	1209	*	941	1209
8	852	1336	0	941	1336
9	852	1477	#	941	1477
C	852	1633	D	941	1633

The attempt to access the remote message playback has to be made after the machine seizes (answers) the line and before the incoming message recording begins, or the generated tones will be on the message playback tape, which will alert the owner that someone is trying to access his machine.

A machine that uses four digits or includes the * and # keys provides much more security—enough to stop all but the most determined hacker. I don't know of any models that has these features now, but sooner or later they will be on the market.

Meanwhile, you might consider making your access code of three random numbers. Don't use the first three digits of your phone number, address, or area or Zip Codes. These are the first combinations an experienced hacker, using a battery-operated Touchtone pad (pocket dialer), will try. "Don't leave home without it," another one of the hacker's ten commandments, refers to the pocket dialer.

VOICE MAILBOXES

Hacking voice mailboxes works in the same basic way as breaking into answering machines. Some computer BBS offer free programs made specifically for hacking voice mail (VM) passwords.

If a hacker has a VM number and he wants to get into its private boxes, he will call it late at night when it isn't busy and activate the program, which will then start dialing password combinations either randomly or sequentially until it opens one and then store that number for later use.

Some VM systems use a four-digit or longer password. Four digits create 10,000 possible combinations, which take a great deal of time to break.

Better systems will disconnect anyone that makes three incorrect attempts at a password. The hacker may hit on a password that is being used just by chance, but this auto-disconnect feature makes it much more difficult and provides more security against hackers.

Voice-mail numbers can be learned by using computers, something like in the movie *War Games*, but with improvements. The telco computer is programmed to look for someone who is dialing many sequential numbers, and when it detects this, it prints the information out on a line printer and alerts the telco security personnel.

The improved system is set to work on a particular exchange and then will dial the last four numbers at random so it does not alert the telco system. It keeps a record of the calls made and the results, such as no answer, disconnect, or the presence of a voice-mail system. Then the password hacking program is used.

If you use voice mail, find out how much security it provides. Does it disconnect a hacker after a certain number of incorrect attempts? Does it keep a record of when it has been accessed? If so, check the record now and then if you have reason to believe someone is trying to get into it.

Accelerated Information, Inc., is a nationwide voice-mail system that has an interesting security feature: if you make a mistake and enter your access code incorrectly, then the computer requires that you enter it again twice. It also will make a record of any incorrect attempts and will advise you automatically, so you will know if someone has been trying to get into your message base.

If you can use a longer password, then do so, remembering to make it of random numbers and not a number someone might assume you would use, as mentioned above. Five digits generate 100,000 possible combinations. One would have to be very determined and spend many hours to break such a password.

A second method of hacking voice mail is to listen to cellular phone frequencies. If someone has your voice mail number and knows you use a cellular phone, he can use a scanner to track your conversation and wait for you to use the VM system. When you punch in the password, the scanner hears the DTMF tones, and a Touchtone decoder connected to the scanner's speaker jack will display them on the panel LEDs. Such a decoder is available commercially, but it is not cheap.

Anyone who is familiar with digital electronics can build a decoder. It is not at all complicated, and the parts cost less than $50. Plans for a decoder can be found in the public library in the electronics section.

An easier method is to use a pager. Tape-record the tones from the scanner, call your pager number, play them into the phone, and the pager will display the number.

Obviously, this technique will also capture calling-card numbers, so consider using direct dial on your cellular phone, and never use or give out your calling-card number over the cellular radio system.

SATELLITE AND MICROWAVE INTERCEPTION

Satellite or microwave interception of phone calls doesn't really apply to most of us, but it is interesting to read about.

Satellite Interception

Satellite phone calls can be intercepted by using a standard TV earth station or a TVRO receiver and a four-foot dish. The satellite receiver's base-band output feeds into a short-wave receiver or scanner antenna connector, and the listener can tune across the band and hear hundreds of phone conversations. However, there is no way to tune in on a particular conversation; it's a matter of hearing whatever is there. Much of the conversation is from big businesses that have branch offices across the country, such as fast-food chains and car-rental agencies, and is very boring, but television stations, newspapers, and wire services use satellite transmissions, and what they have to say can be far from boring. Consider CNN's coverage of the war in the Middle East. There were videotapes of the news crews using a portable four-foot dish antenna to communicate with the networks. With an earth station and

scanner described above, you might have heard all of what they were saying and not just what they were allowed to report.

This process is detailed in *The Hidden Signals on Satellite TV* by Harrington and Cooper, published by Howard Sams & Company.

Microwave Listening

Not so many years ago, all long-distance phone calls traveled over wires strung on telephone poles, but today most of them are relayed by microwave towers. Anyone in the path of these directional microwave signals who has the right equipment can intercept these calls. The receivers are expensive (tens of thousands of dollars), complex, and require sophisticated "demultiplexing" circuits.

Federal intelligence agencies have this equipment and can—and do—listen to the phone conversations that are transmitted over the vast network of microwave relay stations. Overseas calls are routinely listened to by U.S. government agencies—national security considerations again.

The Soviets have the same technology, and one of their embassies just happens to be directly in the path of one of these relay towers. Das vadanya, Ivan . . .

PHONE TRICKS

If someone were to call for an executive of a big company to order a change in phone service, such as a new private line or extension, no one would necessarily know about it until the next bill came,

and even then although things go through channels, it could take some time before he found out that it had been ordered it.

Some big companies have offices in several locations. One person might have an office in two different buildings and have a private line in one and an extension to that line in the other. This is called an outside extension.

If someone knows your private number, he could call the telco and order an outside extension installed in a new property he had "just acquired." A spy could do this and tap your line without having to leave his home. Of course, there is a record of the location of the extension, but it could be a small apartment rented under a phony name.

• • •

Some phones have hook switches that only need to move a quarter inch or so to turn them on. Placing a small square of rubber or plastic under the receiver can hold the line open.

If someone were alone in your office for even a few seconds, he could call a prearranged number and prop the phone receiver up to keep the line open. You probably wouldn't notice it until the next time you used the phone. If he is lucky with his timing, the intruder might be able to listen in on a meeting between you and an important client. The sound will be muffled, but a good amplifier and other audio gear will improve it enough for him to make out what is being said.

Below is another phone trick that sometimes works.

You are Mr. A., the CEO of a medium-size electronics company that makes AC widgets, which is in the process of merging with a company that makes DC widgets. There remain many details to be worked out, and you and the CEO of the other company spend a great deal of time on the phone.

While you are in the middle of doing sixteen other things, your intercom line buzzes. Your secretary tells you she has Mr. B. from the other widget company on the line. You pick up the phone and start talking.

What you don't know is that you are talking to each other through the telephone system of Mr. C., a professional industrial spy who has been hired to get intelligence about the merger. Mr. C. has a tape recorder attached to the phone, and everything you say is being recorded.

What Mr. C. did was to call your office and have his secretary tell your receptionist that she has Mr. B. on the line. Then she called Mr. B. and told his receptionist that she has you on the line. So both of you pick up the phone and start talking, never stopping to think about who called whom.

This has been known to work.

SECURE PHONE COMMUNICATIONS

The above examples provide information on the methods that can be used for phone surveillance. In Part III on finding bugs and wiretaps, there is a chapter devoted to searching phone lines. This information will enable a person to make his inside wiring secure from electronic intrusion—in some cases 100-percent secure; in others, very close to that. Meanwhile, there are other ways of making communications more secure.

The first is to stop using your home or office phone for confidential conversations, i.e., for anything that is important enough to someone to cause him to arrange a phone tap.

Instead, for confidential conversations use a pay phone selected at random and do not use the same one all the time. A quiet place to use a pay phone is hard to find in a large urban area; usually the best place is in the lobby of a large hotel that has a number of phones in a small, quiet room.

If you were in the habit of using such a phone, someone who was following you would know. Real spy stuff, this . . . So what a professional eavesdropper can do is use one of the other phones there, call a prearranged number, then place a small plastic block on the hook switch to hold the line open (as in the preceding example), replace the receiver, and hang an "Out of Order" sign on it. The person at the other end can easily hear you using the phone next to it. Sound farfetched? It's an old trick.

For maximum secrecy, communicate in person or use a computer and a data-encryption program when possible. You can use computer bulletin boards for storing messages to be encrypted.

Phone-scrambling equipment is available that increases the privacy of phone conversations to various levels of security, but they must be used in pairs: the person to whom you are talking has to have the same type and use the same prearranged code as you.

There are solutions to this problem. One readily available, fairly inexpensive device is the phase-inversion device that scrambles sound in such a way that it sounds a little like Donald Duck. This device will keep the average person from knowing what you are saying, but a pro can defeat it. These devices are available from mail-order companies.

Another option is the digital encrypting systems that provide various levels of security, depending on the type of system. The Digital Voice Protection (DVP) system from Motorola provides a high level of security. The following is a semitechnical explanation of how it and the other digital methods work.

First, the sound of your voice goes through a "splatter" or band-pass filter, which 'clips' the bandwidth of the sound. This limits the frequency range and makes it easier to process, similar to the telco system that limits sound from 300 to 3,000 cycles, compared to normal hearing of about 40 to 15,000 cycles.

Then the sound is "sampled." An electronic gate is opened for about 1/10,000 of a second, and the frequency of the sound that passes through the gate is measured. This is the same method used in compact disc (CD) music systems, but where a CD samples the sound 20,000 times a second, the DVP rate is about 7,000. It is less because the bandwidth is narrower.

Each of these samples is then turned into a binary number, a series of ones and zeros, by an integrated circuit called an analog-to-digital converter. Once the sound has been converted to numbers, it is a simple task to scramble these numbers. This is done by both substitution and transposition. The process is simple, but the result is complicated.

The resulting signal, which sounds like the hiss of an FM radio tuned off-station, is sent over the line to the other phone where the process is reversed. The binary numbers are decoded and then fed into a digital-to-analog converter and become your voice again.

Another method of scrambling, called SVX, uses the Data Encryption Standard (DES) developed by IBM for the federal government. It is essentially the same as DVP, except that the algorithm used to scramble the binary numbers is much more complex.

To use the SVX or DVP system, each phone is programmed with the key, using a device that interfaces with a computer (a small PC) called the "keyloader," which has a series of buttons on the front panel that are labeled in hexadecimal, a method of counting based on the number 16 instead of 10. Like the other methods, SVX and DVP require that both parties have the same type of scrambler.

The ultrasecure system that GTE Mobilnet has installed in its cellular system will one day be available to the public, and this will keep your communications secure from anyone except the federal government and other law-enforcement agencies, and possibly some others, but even with the key, a sophisticated computer system that is beyond the means of most eavesdroppers is required to unscramble the transmissions. I don't know when it will be available; some people at GTE won't even admit that it exists. Perhaps if enough people put enough pressure on the feds and GTE it will be soon.

Cellular One is also working on such a system, but the company won't discuss it other than to say it is "on the drawing board."

PART III
FINDING BUGS & WIRETAPS

AN OVERVIEW

Part three is about how to find inside surveillance devices and how to deal with them if any are found. It is divided into two parts: the physical and the electronic search. Electronic searches require equipment that can be expensive and some of which requires experience to use. They are detailed in this part.

The physical search you can do yourself, and if done correctly, it will find practically every type of inside listening device that exists. However, while there is a considerable amount of useful information here, just reading it will not make you an instant expert. There is always the chance you might miss something a pro would have found. If you have the funds, I strongly recommend that you hire a pro.

CONDUCTING A PHYSICAL SEARCH

The examples presented below, as well as the others in the chapters on electronic searches and securing an area, are intended as a guide rather than a complete list. Use your imagination and knowledge of the area to be searched to supplement the list.

First, keep a record of the search and other pertinent information. Make an exploded drawing of the room (as shown in the illustration on page 30) and list all the possible hazards—places a listening device could be hidden. The illustration lists some of them as examples.

Another idea is to photograph the area to be searched; this is particularly important if it is a business with many small offices, a conference room, etc. During the next search, you can compare the photographs to the room to see if anything has been brought into the room(s) that could hide a bug, such as a new plant, picture, books, furniture, and other such places.

Earlier, I suggested that if there is a listening device present, the person on the other end may hear you making the search. Pulling drawers from desks, moving pictures, or checking lamps could give you away. It is better that the listener doesn't know that you are looking, and there are ways of covering the sounds made in the search.

One way is a two-phased search: the silent search and the disguised search. Take a long look at the area and see what can be inspected without making any suspicious noises, make notes in the file, and then do that part first. For a large area with a lot of furniture, bookshelves, and office equipment, consider using small colored inventory labels to mark what has been secured as you cross it off the list.

Some useful tools for a search are pliers, screwdrivers, a magnifying glass, a dentist's mirror, a ruler to measure things for false bottoms or hidden compartments, and a good flashlight. The Mag-Lite and Mini Mag-Lite work well because the beam can be adjusted from wide to narrow, but anything with a very bright beam will do.

Keep in mind what you learned earlier about where devices can be hidden and what to look for—antennas, wires, etc. Before you start, here are some ideas on what to look for.

59A

HAZARD CHART

N

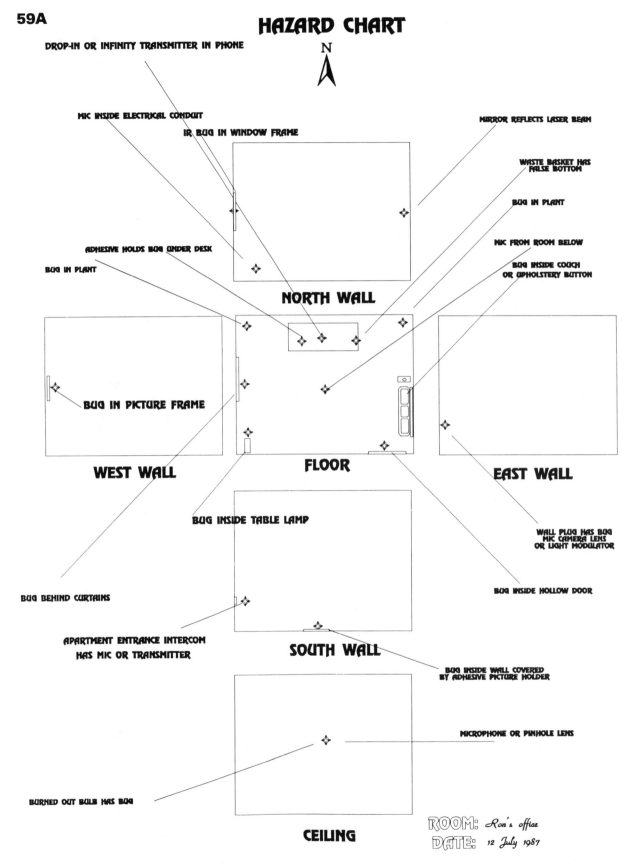

DROP-IN OR INFINITY TRANSMITTER IN PHONE

MIC INSIDE ELECTRICAL CONDUIT

IR BUG IN WINDOW FRAME

MIRROR REFLECTS LASER BEAM

WASTE BASKET HAS FALSE BOTTOM

BUG IN PLANT

MIC FROM ROOM BELOW

ADHESIVE HOLDS BUG UNDER DESK

BUG INSIDE COUCH OR UPHOLSTERY BUTTON

BUG IN PLANT

NORTH WALL

WEST WALL

BUG IN PICTURE FRAME

FLOOR

EAST WALL

BUG INSIDE TABLE LAMP

WALL PLUG HAS BUG MIC CAMERA LENS OR LIGHT MODULATOR

BUG BEHIND CURTAINS

BUG INSIDE HOLLOW DOOR

APARTMENT ENTRANCE INTERCOM HAS MIC OR TRANSMITTER

SOUTH WALL

BUG INSIDE WALL COVERED BY ADHESIVE PICTURE HOLDER

MICROPHONE OR PINHOLE LENS

BURNED OUT BULB HAS BUG

CEILING

ROOM: Ron's office
DATE: 12 July 1987

What Does a Bug Look Like?

Consider a universal truth about inside devices: They all require (or are) a microphone, sometimes called a transducer. Transducer is a generic term for anything that changes energy from one form to another. A microphone changes acoustic energy (sound) to electrical energy. A speaker generally changes electrical to acoustic, but it can work both ways—a speaker can be a microphone.

Obviously, the microphone has to be placed in such a way that it will pick up people's voices inside the room it is in. A room with drapes or curtains, furniture, plants, and wall hangings has better acoustics and better places to hide a bug. A room with bare walls and sparse furnishings doesn't have as many places to hide a listening device.

Placing any type of microphone behind a solid object will mask some of the sound. Anything less solid, such as upholstery fabric, moss, or leaves on a plant, conceals the bug and lets most of the sound in. Certain types of fabrics and foam plastics that are acoustically transparent (such as are used on stereo speakers) will let all the sound through.

With a few rare exceptions, anything a microphone is hidden in will have a small hole to let the sound in. A speaker can also be used, but it is larger and harder to disguise. The most likely place for a speaker being used as a microphone is inside a hollow door where a hole would be seen easily. Regardless of where it is hidden, the wires have to lead to the listening post, and stringing these wires can take time. They obviously have to go through a wall, floor, or ceiling at some location, and this makes a hidden microphone easier to find.

Metallic paint can be used as wires—ordinary wire will go from the microphone along the edge of the carpet to the wall socket, then the paint is sprayed on the wall to lead to the hole. This obviously is then covered with paint that matches what is already on the wall. Look for discoloration because an exact match is unlikely. Such an installation might work in a cheap hotel room or basement maintenance area, but not someone's living room.

To get the wires out of the room and into the listening post, the listener must use a hole that already exists or make a new one. Existing holes are usually behind the plastic plates that cover plug switches, telephone wires, and TV cable or antennas.

Tiny openings can be made from an upstairs apartment, through the floor directly above your ceiling light fixture. Any bits of paint or plaster will fall into the glass cover and not be noticed—until a burned-out bulb is replaced. Holes drilled elsewhere usually leave traces of plaster, etc. Even when small hand drills are used with a vacuum device, some residue usually remains on the floor.

Likely places for a hidden microphone are behind or under furniture that is close to a wall plug, behind drapes, on top of door or window frames, or wedged between them and the wall.

Now, let's look at finding RF devices. How big is a bug? Bugs can be large and easily seen, or they can be so small that you are not likely to find them visually. On "The Man from U.N.C.L.E.," Napoleon Solo used a transmitter inside a pen to talk to people many miles away. No way. On the other hand, a cellular phone could be built into a shoe like the one Maxwell Smart used.

One device, described elsewhere in this book, was made from an old tube-type, table-model AM radio. At the other extreme, a bug inside a martini olive worked. The AM radio bug transmitted for about one-half mile; the olive worked for only a few yards.

The smallest commercially made FM wireless microphone is usually at least 3/8-inch square and 1-inch long and encased in metal to shield it from the NLJD detector described later.

A homemade bug on a printed circuit board is usually no smaller than one-inch square and can be larger.

Batteries

One of the most important things to remember when making a search is to keep a picture of a battery in your mind as you are looking. All bugs have to have power, and if they are not inside something that plugs into the power line, then they must have a battery. If a bug is to operate for more than a few days, the battery is usually larger than the bug.

A very small FM wireless microphone with a range of a hundred feet or so might operate for two or three days on a calculator battery or a week on one AA-cell, but it doesn't have enough power to send its signal through several walls from an inside office to a building across the street. It may reach the floors above and below and the adjacent rooms.

Higher-powered wireless microphones may reach half a block or so under the right conditions, but to last for more than a few days, they need several penlight or one C- or D-size cell. A really large bug with a range of several miles will drain a C-cell in a few hours. To keep transmitting for days or weeks, it requires something on the order of a motorcycle battery.

A number of small batteries can be used to provide the same amount of power as one larger one. A motorcycle battery obviously will not fit inside a hollow door, but a dozen C-cells chained together in parallel can power a wireless microphone for a year.

A D-cell battery will not fit inside a quarter-inch hole drilled in a wall, but dozens of hearing-aid batteries will. It's been done.

Photocells that generate electricity when exposed to light can be used to power a bug. Two small cells could power a small wireless microphone that normally uses a calculator battery. Half a dozen would power a larger wireless microphone. These cells have a surface area of at least one square inch, which has to be exposed to light. Although solar-powered bugs can be used only in certain areas, they have the advantage of never needing the batteries replaced. Inside a ceiling light fixture, certain types of lamp shades, and in a window frame are likely places for a solar-powered device.

What does a bug look like? Look for any kind of electronic device, a small printed circuit board, or a small plastic or metal box or molded rubber block. The block will have a small hole to let the sound into the microphone, and it usually has an antenna wire. The rubber can be molded into shapes other than a block, as well. A glob of caulking compound or putty could hide a bug. Such material would have to contain a battery (which, if seen, would give it away) that might last a week or so. This device has a very short range.

Anything that looks as if it doesn't belong should probably be suspected and examined, and anything that has wires coming out of it should definitely be suspect. Keep in mind that bugs can be disguised as, or hidden in, almost anything.

A bug can be built on a thin, slightly flexible type of circuit board using very small components, such as surface-mount chips, which are smaller than ordinary integrated circuits.

The battery can be made from a number of small individual cells that are spread out over the board. Such a device can be less than a quarter-inch thick and can fit in the space between the spine and cover of a large book.

Antennas

In an episode of "The Equalizer" on TV, an RF bug about two inches square was placed inside the limousine of the bad guy, and the sound it transmitted was heard clearly several blocks away. A bug of this size could have such a range, but not without the one thing missing from the bug on the show: the antenna.

Even a high-power bug isn't going to transmit very far without an antenna, which can be anything made of metal. A strip of aluminum foil, a curtain rod (an excellent antenna), the brackets that hold a lamp shade, wire that holds a picture on a wall, a metal bar for hanging clothes, springs inside furniture and mattresses, a filing cabinet—literally anything made of any kind of metal—will work, as long as it is not grounded. Keep this in mind when searching for a hidden antenna.

A later chapter contains some examples of places that bugs have been hidden. Keep these in mind also. Start with the windows, which are one of the best places for the bugs described above because the glass doesn't interfere with the signal as walls can. Check curtains and drapes. Stand on a chair or ladder so you can look down at the top of the rods. Use a flashlight. Look in the window frame for a solar cell or infrared transmitter. A bug could be painted over to make it less noticeable.

Check on the outside of the glass for anything stuck to it. Have a look from the outside if possible. A contact microphone could be placed on the glass, with fine wires hidden in the shingles or behind a downspout or even painted over, and lead to a nearby listening post or to a transmitter hidden in the grass or buried with the antenna just below the grass. Look closely for tiny wires or places where the paint is discolored and doesn't match.

Then look up from below. Small bugs can be hidden in the folds of the drapes. Shine a small flashlight from behind the tops of the drapes and look for the silhouette of a listening device. The metal hooks that hold the drapes to the rods could be used as an antenna.

Look behind the brackets that hold the rods to the wall. Open or close the curtains if necessary. Tiny relay bugs can be hidden inside the plastic handles on the drawstrings of drapes and venetian blinds.

Lamps are another likely place for bugs. Some shades are made from two layers of material, one inside the other. A small bug could be dropped inside from a small hole in the top. Turn the lamp on and look closely for shadows near the bottom.

A small, or not so small, bug can be hidden behind a picture on a wall. Use a flashlight and look very closely. If it is hung with wires, look for another wire attached to them. Use a mirror and look along the edges.

Plants can easily conceal snooping devices. Look carefully.

Check underneath desks, chairs, and other furniture. Crawl under them and use the flashlight. Look for signs of fabric having been cut and sewed up or tacks pulled loose and replaced. Look closely at the buttons on the upholstery to see if there seems to be a difference in color, if one looks newer than the others. Large upholstery buttons are one of the best places for hiding small bugs. The fabric lets the sound through, and with an upholsterer's front button hook, the bugs can be switched in a few seconds.

Of course, this requires that the spy know the kind of fabric used and be able to obtain the same kind. Because of their small size, they have a short life, but if they have to transmit only a few yards, they might last a week. This is a long shot, but it has been done. If someone wants information badly enough, they will do whatever is necessary to get it.

Get a ladder and replace a bulb in the ceiling light fixture. Have a good look here; this is another favorite hiding place. Look for scraps of paint or plaster from someone having drilled a hole from above. Make a note of any such opening.

Bugs have been built into burned-out light bulbs. There is enough space for a large bug inside one, and it has a constant power supply. In a fixture with a number of bulbs, a single burned-out one might not be replaced for months. It's one of those little things that people never seem to get around to.

If you have a ceiling light fixture, then the apartment below you probably does also. Check the carpeting in the center of the room for anything irregular, a bulge or soft spot, or a sound hole. Use a magnifying glass and flashlight.

If you have a smoke detector, replace the battery and have a close look. With the electronic components that belong there, it may be hard to tell if there is a bug inside. Look for a microphone. If in doubt, compare it with another of the same model or replace it.

Look closely at your books, using the flashlight, for any signs that the material on the spine has been tampered with, such as a tiny hole to let sound into a hearing-aid microphone.

Quietly remove a few of the larger ones and look behind the others with a mirror and flashlight. Look along the tops for signs that dust has been disturbed.

Check the carpet all the way around the edges to see if it can be peeled back; a small bug can be hidden there, as can wires for a microphone.

Disguising the Sound of a Search

Anything that makes noise will help to cover the sound of a search, but some noises are better than others. A vacuum cleaner is one good cover. Much can be done while the carpets are being steam-cleaned. An electric drill makes a good cover. Find something to make some holes in, put up some new book shelves, do some remodeling, have a loud party.

Repainting, having the walls cleaned or repapered, or rearranging furniture all help to conceal the sounds made in searching.

Different sounds can be used for different parts of the search. For example, removing a wall plug cover requires the loudest sounds you can generate because you are making mechanical noise very close to the microphone. After arranging suitable noise, as quietly as possible, remove the covers from wall plugs, switches, and cable TV. Keep in mind all the things that can be in such a location: a microphone or the plastic tube from a microphone, a pinhole lens from a TV camera, an RF bug, a wireless microphone, or a light modulator. A wall plug cover is a universal place for surveillance devices. In a plug or switchbox, there should be nothing else but the plug (outlet) or switch.

The plug will have either one or two heavy wires (number 12 or 14 and usually white and black) on each side of the plug and sometimes a bare copper wire that connects to a screw on the metal box. This is a ground wire.

A switch will have two, possibly three (on a three-way switch) wires and the bare ground wire. Look closely. Use the flashlight and mirror. No small wires or anything else should be there.

If the TV cable comes in through a hole drilled in floor or wall, you can't see much, but if it enters from a box, look inside. There should be nothing inside it except the cable—no electronic components, other wires, or splices.

Now check the place where the phone wires come in, usually in one of two ways. Either a small four-wire cable will enter through a small drilled hole, or there will be a switchbox with a plastic cover like the plugs and switches, and a modular jack in the cover.

If there is a plate, remove it and look inside. There may be a small beige-colored cable with four wires inside, which have red, green, black, and yellow insulation. Or there may be two single wires of other colors. If so, look for a large cable inside the wall. Use a mirror and flashlight to see if you can find it. It may be inside the wall and hard to see. Make a mental note of the type of cable.

Every book you have should be removed from the shelves and opened to see if it has been replaced by a hollowed-out one. Remember that large books can have a bug inside the spine if it is loose, like many old law books, some of which are seldom used. Then use a flashlight and check the empty shelves carefully.

Quietly remove pictures, bulletin boards, and other wall hangings and have a close look. Bugs can be built into the frames.

There are bugs that are long and thin and will fit inside the wall through a small hole.

The hole can be hidden by an old, unused adhesive picture hanger that has a tiny hole for the microphone. The batteries, small hearing-aid types that are chained, can supply a low power bug for weeks or months.

Hollow doors have enough space for a large bug and a long antenna. A number of small batteries chained together, as in the above example, will fit inside, and a speaker, used as a microphone, can be wedged inside with foam rubber to hold it in place. The surface of the door, which vibrates with

sound, acts as a sounding board for the speaker. No sound hole is needed.

Look at the top of the doors for evidence of tampering—e.g., a hole that has been covered over, patched, or even left open. If you found a bug inside a door, you would not be the first person to do so.

Upholstered furniture should be closely examined for tears in the fabric, tacks that are loose, or labels or stickers that could conceal an opening into which a bug could be inserted. There is a lot of space inside furniture to accommodate a large bug and many batteries, and the springs make a good antenna. If in doubt, have it reupholstered or replace it.

Typewriters and printers can also hide bugs. To wire them to the power line takes time, but a small battery-operated bug can be hidden inside the case from the top. You know what to look for.

Phones can be unplugged and examined, but since there are phone bugs that are as small as a pea, they might be missed. Have them examined by an expert or just replace them.

Now consider the possibility of a Trojan horse. Any kind of gift could contain a bugging device. A desk pen-and-pencil holder, decoration or sculpture, wall hanging, or a plant.

A gift that plugs into the wall outlet should be removed from the area, taken apart, and checked physically and electronically, using equipment described in the next section. Table lamps are one of the best places to hide a listening device. A typical ceramic base lamp could hide a multitude of devices.

Anything that is "accidentally" left behind by a visitor, client, friend, etc., should be removed from the area and checked out or placed inside sound-absorbing material and put in a storage area or closet.

Briefcases can have bugs built into them that you can't see without tearing them apart. They can also conceal small tape recorders with voice-actuated remote control (VOX) switches and can be easily modified to record for eight to twelve hours.

The man had a legitimate claim. There were witnesses who saw him pushing the wheelbarrow up the hill when it fell on him. The insurer tried to deny the claim and refused to pay him disability, even though several doctors said he was injured. He threatened to sue and showed them that he knew enough about civil law to do so.

The insurance representatives called him in for a meeting, after which he "forgot" his attache case, which contained a VOX tape recorder. When he retrieved it and listened to the tape, he learned that the insurance company was willing to "buy him off" rather than fight him in court.

A week later he left their office with a check for $5,000 in his pocket. They tried to cheat him out of what he was legally entitled to, and he fought back.

TYPES OF EQUIPMENT USED FOR ELECTRONIC SEARCHES

In this section, we will examine countersurveillance devices that are used for finding bugs and how they are used. Some are inexpensive and easy to use, while others cost thousands of dollars and require an experienced operator.

The Bug Detector

A bug detector is a small battery-operated wide-band radio receiver that will detect RF bugs over a wide range of frequencies, typically from 1 to 1,000 mc. They vary from shirt-pocket-size to about 4 by 6 inches.

Most of these units are not tunable. They receive the whole range without needing to be tuned. Outside stations can be eliminated by reducing the sensitivity, or the search can be done in the early morning when there are fewer commercial stations on the air.

Some of the better models have a verify mode. When the LEDs indicate a signal, the mode is changed to verify, and the signal it has detected comes through the speaker or headphones. This tells you what you have found and eliminates false signals.

These detectors run from about one hundred to several thousand dollars. Capri Electronics makes the model TD-53 with the verify mode, and it has optional probes for detecting infrared light, carrier-current (wireless intercoms), and video cameras.

I tested the TD-53. A very low-output wireless microphone was hidden inside a retail store while I was outside. I found it in less than a minute.

To use a bug detector, walk through the area several times holding the antenna probe at different angles and poking it into corners and close to furniture and other appointments. When it picks up a signal the red LED indicator on the front panel lights up and changes as you get closer to the transmitter.

Then you can switch to the verify mode. If the speaker is being used, you'll hear the squealing of feedback. If using the headphones, you will hear the sounds you are making as you move around. Using headphones prevents the listener from knowing that the device has been located—there is no feedback for them to hear.

A good bug detector used carefully will find any RF transmitter in the search area with the exception of high microwave devices (which are rare) the burst transmitter (even rarer), and possibly the low-frequency-type mentioned in a Part I. Some bug detectors cover low frequency; some do not.

Microwave Detectors

A microwave detector is the same as the bug detector, but it works on (receives) microwave frequencies, and some models have special filters to block signals on nonmicrowave frequencies that could interfere. The coverage of most of these is about 800 mc. to about 2 or 3 gc., and they will not detect the 10 to 11 gc. types or some video cameras that operate on about 4 gc.

Ultrasonic Sound Generators

All RF bugs (wireless microphones, converted cordless phones, etc.), IR transmitters, and tape recorders require microphones to pick up sounds. Most can be found or jammed by using ultrasonic sound.

The USS device generates two separate signals that sweep through the range at different speeds so they produce all combinations of the two frequencies.

When these USS waves strike a microphone, they cause it to oscillate (vibrate), which jams it and makes it deaf, and some types emit a whistling sound, which gives away the location.

This works on most but not all microphones. For it to work, the microphones must have a frequency response that goes beyond audio and into the USS area. Carbon microphones, for example, and the microphones in some tape recorders do not respond to the USS generator.

A jamming system called "The Exterminator" is available from CSI.

Tape Recorder Detectors

All but a few cheap tape recorders generate an ultrasonic sound called a bias, usually at about 100,000 cycles. A device that finds a hidden tape recorder by detecting this sound is available from Sherwood Communications and CSI. If a recorder were to be left in an attache case, as in the previous example, this would most likely find it.

Scanners

Scanners are useful in countersurveillance work. They don't work as fast as bug detectors, but they have the advantage of providing you with the frequency that a found bug transmits on. This is useful in making a profile. Also, some scanners cover frequencies that many bug detectors do not.

The AR-3000 is recommended, as it will pick up everything from DC to infrared. Actually the coverage is 100 kc. to 2,036 mc.—which is continuous, meaning that nothing is locked out. Because of its wide coverage, it will detect any RF device except the burst and some microwave transmitters.

Most scanners have two modes: scan and search. Using the search mode, the operator can set a high and low frequency limit, and the unit then scans through this area over and over, looking for a signal. Unfortunately, when it finds a station, it stops and stays there until it is reset or the station stops transmitting.

The AR-3000 has the search lock-out feature that no other current scanner has. You can set it to search through a certain part of its coverage and lock out the unwanted signals. Up to forty-eight separate signals can be deleted, so the scanner can search for bugs without the operator having to reset it constantly.

For example, if you wanted to search from 160 to 165 mc., an area used by the federal government for bugs and body microphones (wires), the scanner would stop on the NOAA National Weather Service stations on 162.45, 162.55, etc. The lock-out feature causes the unit to pass over these stations and continue looking for bugs.

Here are two ways to use a scanner. For the first, you need a phone that has an infinity transmitter (usually called "answer back") built in, such as the Panasonic KX-T2432 mentioned above. Set the scanner to cover a particular area you want to search

and lock out the unwanted signals. Turn on a radio in the room you are searching, plug a speaker with a long cord into the scanner's external speaker jack, and lead this into another room. Place the speaker next to the phone.

If the scanner finds a bug, it will stop on its frequency and hear the music from the radio, which comes out the speaker beside the phone. All you need to do is call the phone and activate the answer-back feature to see if you hear the music.

The second method can be used if you don't have an AR-3000, or if there are too many interfering stations, such as those for pagers, which are everywhere in a downtown area. It isn't unattended, but you can use it while doing something else.

Set the scanner beside you where you can easily reach the panel buttons. Plug headphones into the phone jack, hang them around your neck, and sit back and watch videos.

When the scanner hears a bug, you will hear your TV sound coming from the headphones. To search a different room, just use an external antenna placed in that room, turn on a radio, and go back to watching television.

To be thorough, search the entire range, but there are a number of smaller areas to start with. The best place to start is the FM broadcasting band, where most wireless microphones transmit. FM is from 88 to 108 mc., but some wireless microphones can be adjusted to work slightly above or below FM, so search from 80 to 115 or so.

One of the most difficult bugs to find is set to transmit near the sound portion of a TV channel. Because of the close proximity, these are often covered by the buzzing that TV sound signals generate and can be quite hard to find.

The use of such device is called "snuggling," and it signifies the work of an experienced spy. The frequencies for VHF TV channels are listed in Appendix D, along with a list of common frequencies used by wireless microphones and other such devices.

The military aircraft and operations band, from 235 to 420 mc., is a good place to look. Until a few years ago, scanners (or any receivers) that tuned this area were uncommon. The military surplus URR-35 and R278 covered most of this band, but were hard to find. This made for a safe area in which to place RF bugs, and they are still being used there.

If nothing is found in these areas, then do the continuous search with whatever scanner you have available, but if the coverage is less than the AR-1000, you will be missing some areas in which bugs can work.

The Hunter

The scanner methods discussed above are effective, but here is something that does it one better, the Hunter. Made by CSI in Santa Clara, California, it is a modified ICOM R-7000 communications receiver with a specially made controller that sits on top.

To search for an RF bug, you place a second unit called a scout in the room(s) to be searched. The scout emits a 4,000-cycle tone that will be picked up by any bug in the room.

Meanwhile, the R-7000 (an excellent receiver) is searching from 25 to 2,000 mc., listening for the tone emitted by the scout. The controller causes the R-7000 to skip any signal that does not contain that tone, and because of extensive modifications, it hears AM, FM, and single sideband (SSB) without requiring you to manually switch modes and redo the search in each one.

The Hunter searches continuously until it finds the tone, which means it has found a bug. It then stops and stores that frequency. You can set it up in your office and go home, leaving the Hunter to do the searching for you. It's great for remote-control bugs. It also can trigger an audible alarm, so you can call using a phone, as in our example above, to see if it has found anything.

The Scan-Lock

The scan-lock is a special scanning receiver that can be computer programmed to overlook all of the known transmitters in the area in which it is being used. In other words, it will lock out commercial radio and TV stations, amateur radio and business band systems, etc. Once programmed, it will look for bugs continuously until it is reset.

Scan-lock was supposedly developed by British intelligence and has a wide coverage, 100 kc. to 2 gc., which it can scan through in about six minutes. Once classified technology, the scan-lock is now

available commercially, but it is hard to find. Try Sherwood. It has one now and then.

The Spectrum Analyzer

The spectrum analyzer is a useful device available for detecting RF bugs, but it also is one of the most expensive. It is a sophisticated receiver with a wide coverage that displays what it receives on a computer screen. Depending on the model, the screen can display an area, called a window, several megacycles wide.

These signals are displayed as vertical blips, which by their size and shape indicate information about the signal: mode (FM, AM), frequency, and other useful data. To use it, the operator sets the analyzer to display a portion of the radio spectrum to be searched and watches the screen for signals.

The AX-700 analyzer, available from EEB, covers 50 to 900 mc., has 100 memory channels, and sells for around $800. It also has optional coverage of 100 kc. to 50 mc. for a modest $249, and it can be interfaced to a computer via the built-in RS-232 port. Sensitivity is comparable to better communications receivers, in other words, quite good.

The Hewlett-Packard (HP) model 71210C receives and displays almost the entire radio spectrum, from 100 cycles to 22 gc. with optional coverage to 325 gc. This coverage will find any surveillance transmitter. It has a color multiplexed screen and all the bells and whistles one could want. Base price is about $80,000. You probably get a discount if you buy two.

Tektronix also makes spectrum analyzers, and like the HP, its top-of-the-line models are of excellent quality and comparable price. Both companies also have less expensive models.

Most two-way-radio repair shops have spectrum analyzers, and if you know someone in that business, you might be able to borrow one to sweep for RF listening devices. But read the manual first; they are a bit more complicated than scanners.

The spectrum analyzer will detect a burst transmitter, but this takes time, depending on the model. Some have a wider window than others, and some can be programmed to search different areas of the spectrum.

A continuous sound causes the memory chips in the burst device to fill, which then prompts it to transmit. When it does, the spectrum analyzer receives the transmission, and the display reveals the frequency. Some models have a storage memory that freezes the image on the screen.

Using surface-mount technology, a burst transmitter that could store about ten to twenty minutes of sound would be about the size of two 35mm film boxes. The exact size would depend upon the skill of the person who builds it and the parts available.

The Nonlinear Junction Detector

Bugs are made (in part) from transistors and diodes, which are made from layers of different types of silicon (P-type and N-type), and the point at which these layers meet is called a junction. One of the characteristics of these junctions is that when they are subjected to microwaves of a certain frequency, they reflect back microwaves of different frequencies, called harmonics.

A nonlinear junction detector (NLJD) floods the area to be searched with microwaves, and if a bug is present, it detects these harmonics from the transistors and alerts the operator by registering on a panel meter or sounding an alarm. The NLJD looks somewhat like a metal detector. The main part can be clipped to a belt or shoulder sling, and the probe is swept over the walls, etc.

During construction of the U.S. Embassy in Moscow, the Soviets buried hundreds of cheap diodes in the walls. Then when the countersurveillance crews tried to use their NLJDs, they were so swamped with false readings that they couldn't find the real bugs. Clever, those Russians.

One of the features of the NLJD is that it can detect a bug that is not turned on (remote-control activated) or has a dead battery, as well as a wireless intercom and anything that has transistors.

Unfortunately, a bug that is well-shielded (in a metal case) will be missed by the NLJD, and the device also tends to detect other types of junctions. More than once a wall has been ripped out to find a bug only to discover a corroded plumbing solder joint. Though not perfect, the NLJD works in the hands of an experienced operator, but it is not for amateurs.

A NLJD sells for about $15,000, and I have heard that an improved type is being developed.

The Frequency Counter

Another device for finding bugs is the frequency counter or meter. Portable pocket-size counters, available from Optoelectronics, range from about $119 to $375 and cover from 10 cycles to 2.4 gc.

When the antenna is in the presence of an RF field (radio waves), it detects it, counts the number of cycles per second that it is receiving, and displays the frequency on the front panel. The frequency counter is as sensitive as some scanners, very effective, much faster, and has the added advantage of indicating the operating frequency of the detected device. This may tell you something about the person who placed it, useful in building a profile, which is detailed later.

To use, turn the unit on and walk around the area being searched, as if you were using a bug detector, and watch the panel display to see if it stabilizes, i.e., displays a number that doesn't keep changing. Then program a scanner to the same reading to verify it and see what you hear. Use an earphone or the squealing feedback sound will tell the listener you have found and now own his bug.

• • •

As you have seen, the cost of countersurveillance equipment is considerable. A first-rate spectrum analyzer, NLJD, and a few other sophisticated gadgets can add up to $100,000. This equipment is fascinating and fun to use (if a little pricey for most people), but the vast majority of the RF bugs used by anyone, even the pros and the government, can be found with the moderately priced frequency counter from Optoelectronics or the TD-53 bug detector and a shortwave receiver.

SEARCHING THE PHONE LINES

As mentioned in a previous section, a phone-listening device can be direct (a wire connected to the line leading to the listening post) or remote (a RF transmitter connected to the line, which radiates the signal to the listener without wires).

In either case a wire will be connected to your line. If it is, then you can almost always find it. The few exceptions will be explained later.

You will need the tools used in the physical search, an ohmmeter and something to connect across phone lines to listen in. It will be necessary to get to the place at which the phone lines all come together, the 66 block or other connection panel, possibly several times. Allow an hour or two for the search.

In the physical search, you made a note of the type of cable used. If it is the four-wire type that goes to a modular jack, remove it and look at the back for anything that does not belong there. There are line-powered bugs as small as a pea that can be hidden there. They have two thin wires connected across the screws that have the red and green wires connected to them.

If there is a large twenty-five-pair (or larger) cable, is it close enough that you could splice a wire to it? If so, then someone else could do so.

Tracing Wires

In larger office and department buildings, either type of cable will probably go straight down, inside the wall, to the basement, so there may not be any way to get to it. Other buildings may have the wire running through the walls over doorways, along halls, etc. Follow it as far as you can.

Any wires branching off the line should be connected inside a standard four-wire telco block or modular jack, or held together with small plastic connecting devices such as wire nuts or scotch-locks.

A splice, wires twisted together and left bare or covered with tape, will have been made by someone other than a telco installer—such as a wiretapper. If you find a splice, follow it as far as possible to see where it goes, but leave it alone for now.

A small line-powered bug may be wrapped inside a piece of tape or hidden behind a connection block or inside a short piece of plastic phone cable insulation that looks like a wire that was connected, then cut off. Remember that anything that small will have a range of a hundred feet at best.

Remove any tape and connection blocks you find and look inside and behind them. Just as above, the only thing that should be there is plastic: four screws and the two or four wires inside the cable with red, green, yellow, and black insulation.

Also look for a coil of wire that will be an inductive tap or "pick-up." It can be of any size, as small as a thimble, or a flat plastic plate several inches across. Whatever its size, it will have a wire coming out of it that leads elsewhere or is attached to an RF bug. Look for a battery.

Inductive pick-ups are usually placed close to a phone where there is more magnetism to pick up. The flat plate type is placed under the phone, and smaller ones have a suction cup to hold them on the receiver. They are seldom used along a phone line because they don't work very well and easily pick up interference from power lines and many kinds of appliances, motors, etc., but they do exist.

In your search, you might find a small circuit board about one inch square with electronic parts and a small plastic block about a quarter-inch square that has four small slide switches This is the dual inline package (DIP) switch. It will have four wires, two red and two green. This is a radio frequency interference (RFI) filter used when transmissions from commercial radio stations get into the line. It is not a listening device.

When you reach the place at which the line disappears into a wall or floor, pick up the search from the other end.

If you're searching an apartment on the ground floor and the connection block is in the basement, you can push a stiff wire, such as a coat hanger, into the hole, which you may be able to see from inside the basement. Another trick is to shine a very bright light into the hole. This makes it easier to find the wire again.

Some buildings often have the connection panel on a basement wall where anyone can get to it. If so, look for apartment numbers beside the pairs of terminals. If there are none, follow the wires and look for tags hanging on them with the numbers. Also look for a ceramic or metal block about four by six inches, a single-pair station protector (SPSP), which may have the apartment number written on it. Check it out and follow the wires as far as possible.

Newer buildings usually have a distribution closet in the basement and sometimes a smaller one on each floor called a floor closet. These usually (but not always) are in areas that are hard to get to and sometimes are locked. If so, perhaps a maintenance person will let you in, or you might find a way to get past the lock.

The connection panel(s) may be locked with a TORX security screw, which is round and has a hex-shaped opening in the top. These can be opened with a special tool called a TORX wrench, available from Bit Connection.

When you have accessed the block, look again at the rows of connections to see if they are labeled with the apartment numbers, or there may be a written list inside the block cabinet or elsewhere in the closet. Make a note of the colors of the wires in the block. The twenty-five-pair cable has ten different colored wires inside it, and if this is the type of cable inside the wall box in your unit, then the wires coming into the block should have the same number of colors, not just red and green.

These colors are in two groups of five: blue, orange, green, brown, and slate; and white, red, black, yellow, and violet. Each line will have one color from each group. This makes twenty-five combinations.

If a larger cable is used, fifty or one hundred pairs, the wires will be divided into binder groups each with twenty-five pairs, using the same color codes and separated by wrapping them in a color-coded string or ribbon.

If, however, they are multicolored and the cable in your unit is the small four-wire type, then one of two things is true. First, there is a large cable back inside the wall where you couldn't see it. If the four-wire cable enters through a drilled hole rather than a box with a plastic cover, you won't be able to see the large cable without making a hole in the wall.

The other possibility is that there is a floor closet, a small distribution closet on some or all floors of the building. The small wires will go from it to each unit, and a large cable will connect the floor closet to the main panel in the basement.

A floor closet is a likely place for a tape recorder or remote phone bug.

If the lines are not labeled, then you have to trace your line.

The easiest way to do this is to just leave the phone off the hook and, when the beeping sound stops, turn on a radio near the phone. This gives you a sound to listen for.

Next, you need something to use to listen to all of the lines that come into the block. A lineman's test set is ideal, as it has a listen-only switch. If you are using an ordinary phone, connect alligator clips (available at any ham radio or electronics store for about a dollar) through a small capacitor to the red and green wires of the phone. The reason for this is to reduce the click sound—if you connect across a line that someone is using, he or she will probably not hear it. There is no reason to cause that person to think someone has tapped his/her line.

If you are using a phone that has a modular plug, buy an extra cord that has the plug on one end and small metal "spade" clips on the other. The clips connect to the screw terminals on the alligator clips.

Now go back to the main closet block and start checking the pairs by connecting the two alligator clips to each of them. It does not matter which clip goes to which terminal. Some blocks (usually older ones) have pairs of large brass screws in two or more vertical rows. Other blocks have rows of small curved clips to which the wires go. These are called insulation displacement connectors. A small device called an impact tool is used to push the wire into the clip, make the connection, and cut off the loose end of the wire.

Try them until you hear your radio playing and note any numbers beside the terminals or count how far the line is from the top pair. Look closely at your pair of wires and the terminals to which it goes. There should be only two pairs of wires: one coming in from the outside and the one going to your phone.

On an older block, in an old building, the incoming wires are usually of a different size and color—larger with black insulation. In the newer blocks that use the clips, each of the two clips have one wire for the line to the phone, and the incoming line usually enters the block from the back. If there are more than two pairs of wires connected to any of the terminals then the third is probably a tap. See where it goes.

The black and yellow wires in the two-pair cable are never used. If there is a second line, it will have its own separate four-wire cable. If you see black and yellow wires attached to yours, it will be a bridging tap.

Look behind the block, if possible, for the same things as before—a splice, tape, coil of wire, etc. Also check that the block is securely bolted to the wall and that there is no evidence that it has been removed and replaced, such as plaster dust or paint chips on the floor. Also look for places on the wall at the edge of the block that have been repainted so the colors don't match. Remember the earlier example of using metallic paint as wires? Look for this as well.

In both new and old buildings, there might be a small box on the wall near the telco block, which may have the telco name on it. It is big enough to hide a small tape recorder, which can have extra batteries, be modified to record for ten hours or so, and be operated by a dropout relay. If you see such a box, open it and see what is inside. If it and the telco block are mounted on a wall made of wood or plasterboard, find out what is on the other side. It can have a jumper wire attached to the back of the telco block from behind the wall, which you otherwise would not have found, as you might not have paid any attention to the other box.

The next step is to measure the resistance of the line. Meters that will do this are available from any electronics supply house. An analog meter costs about $35. A decent digital meter is available from Jameco for $40. The instruction book that comes with it contains all the information you need to use it.

There are also products that will do this without your needing to learn how to use the ohmmeter, such as the Tap Trap for about $100, but they use LEDs instead of meters. The meter is more accurate.

First a short primer on Ohm's law, which is the most basic law in electronics. An analogy that compares a phone system to a water tank on a tower is useful. Gravity makes water flow to a lower level; the electronic "gravity" that makes electricity flow is voltage or electrical pressure. The flowing of the water or electricity is current, and a valve that controls how much water or current flows is resistance. High resistance is like a closed valve, no water or current flows; whereas an open valve (no resistance) allows as much water or current to flow as the pipe or wire can handle.

Measuring Line Resistance

Telephones work by being connected with wires through which a small electric current flows. Wires have resistance to this flow of current; the longer the wires, the greater the resistance. (Technically, it is impedance, which is a combination of resistance and capacitive and inductive reactance).

Any device electrically attached to a line between the point at which the line enters the house (SPSP) or building (block) and the phone inside will make a change in the resistance of the line and, unlike downline taps, can be easily found with an ohmmeter.

Before you leave the 66 block, disconnect both the incoming line and the line going up to your phone. When you get back, unplug your phone and anything else that is on the line—answering machine, computer modem, etc.

Set your meter to one of the higher scales (R x 10K ohms or R x 100K ohms), then short the leads together, and watch the needle to make sure it reads zero. (This is not necessary with a digital meter.) There is a small knob marked "ohms adjust" to set it to zero if necessary.

Connect the test leads from the meter to the red and green wires in the phone block or modular jack. The other end of the wires is not (or should not be) connected to anything, so there is infinite resistance. On the analog meter, the needle should not move.

If the needle first went toward the zero end and then slowly started back the other way, something is on the line; this is a capacitor charging. If it moves, make a note of the reading.

Different brands of digital meters have different displays. Read the instructions to see what a very high or infinity measurement should read.

The next step is to short the red and green wires by twisting the bare ends together or connecting another short wire across them. Take your meter and go back to the closet. Set the meter on the lowest range, usually R x 1 or R x 10 ohms, and measure the same wires, still connected to the block terminals.

What you are now measuring, of course, is the resistance of the loop of wire. One thousand feet of number 22 wire has a resistance of 16 ohms, so if your phone is 500 feet from the block, or on about the thirtieth floor, that's about what the meter should read. If it is more than 16 ohms, there is likely a series tap on the line. Check the meter, make sure the ohms adjustment is set right, and try it again.

There is one more check to make. With both pairs disconnected, measure across the terminals on the block, from the line in to the line out terminals on one side and then the other. They should read a dead short. If not, then a series device is hidden inside or behind the block.

If you got a high reading in the first test, measure across the terminals the other way. The reading should be infinity. If it is less, a parallel device is inside or behind the block.

If the readings aren't normal, then either you missed something while searching the line, or whatever is connected to the line is in a place you couldn't get to. If there is a floor closet, check it out the same as the main one.

Sometimes the lines will go down an elevator shaft or through a maintenance area. See what you can find out from the maintenance people or find out who did the inside wiring. Most of it is done by private contractors since the Bell system break-up. There may be labels on the block with the company name on them.

The other possibility is that someone got into the cable from one of the units and placed the tap, and unless you can get into every apartment that the cable serves, you aren't going to find it. There is, however, a way to destroy it described later.

Once the phone wires leave the 66 block, they become the telco's property and responsibility. This is the "point of demarcation." Usually, there will be another block that contains fuses or overload protectors. If you can get to it, check it out the same as the 66 block.

The Reflectometer

At this point, you have done everything you can do. Put everything back the way it was. Now you have two more choices.

The first is to call in an expert who will use a device called the "time domain reflectometer" (TDR). The TDR is a sophisticated and very expensive electronic device that will send a signal down a pair of wires in such a way that a break in the cable or another wire that is connected to it will reflect part of the signal back to the unit. The qualities of the reflected signal are such that the TDR can measure the distance from the unit to the break or tap and display it on the screen. Hewlett Packard has a TDR for only $13,000. HP doesn't make anything cheap, but it makes some of the best electronic equipment on the market. There are other brands on the market in the $2,000 range.

Gremlins, Martians, and Ghosts

The other option is to have the phone company do the search. This can be an interesting experience. The security division of the telco that deals with wiretapping does not like to talk to the public. If you call the telco and try to get through to security, they will tell you this. You must persist until you succeed.

Then you will be screened. They are used to people whose phones have gremlins in them, whose departed husbands or wives are trying to contact them but the operator won't put the call through, and whom the Martians call late at night. You will immediately be classed as such a person until you can convince them you are a rational human being who does not use LSD very often.

Now the obvious reason you are calling them is because you believe there is a tap on your line. Telco personnel do not like that word. They get real serious about it. I called Pacific Bell—many times—to see how its personnel handled such requests. I carefully explained that I was writing a book; I made a point of telling them this (again, many times), and finally someone said he would have a representative call me back.

Several days later a gruff-sounding gent using a speaker phone called and said, "So you think someone has tapped your line, eh?" with an undisguised mixture of sarcasm and condescension.

I explained that I was writing a book and I was reasonably rational, but he was very uncooperative and refused to tell me anything about how the telco would go about such a search, but after repeatedly asking the same question, he finally admitted that, yes, Pacific Bell would make such a search, and, yes, it would arrange to have my line physically disconnected at its end to make resistance measurements. I asked if he would tell me how the line is routed from any given phone to the central office, to make it easier to estimate the line resistance, but he didn't want to talk about it. When he hung up, he did not say anything like, "Thank you for calling Pacific Bell." Like I said, talking to the telco is an interesting experience.

So if you decide to have the telco test your line for taps, you can get it done but expect a little reluctance. Some professional debuggers are well known to the telco, and they can cut through the red tape.

DOWN LINE

Once the wires leave the overload protection system, they go into a heavy plastic tube that is filled with a jellylike substance to keep moisture out, which leads to the underground conduits or to a telephone pole in an alley.

Earlier, I said down-line taps are difficult to find, especially inductive taps. In the above test, the resistance of the wires from your phone to the block was a known quantity—you knew what the meter should read. With a down-line tap, there is no known quantity.

Even if it were measured when the phone was first installed, the resistance can change from new cables being installed, lines being rerouted from one switching office (SO) to another, or other factors. Even variations in temperature change the resistance of wire.

An inductive tap is not physically connected to the line and does not change the resistance. It could have an insignificant effect on the impedance of the line, but a change in temperature of a few degrees would have as great an effect. One "expert" from a large company that sells countersurveillance equipment told me that he has a machine that will "find any phone tap no matter what kind or where it is." No way. The real experts will tell you about line resistance and take measurements for later comparison, or use the TDR.

I also said earlier that down-line taps are rare. The first place to access the line after it leaves the building is on a telephone pole or junction point. A wiretapper who wants to climb a pole to tap a line has two ways to do it. First, he can use an extension ladder, but this will attract attention, especially without a telco truck on the scene. The other way is to use climbers and a safety belt. These cost about $300, and the climbers are not easy to use. It takes some practice. Take my word for it. A lineman's test set will add about a hundred or more to the cost. This eliminates most amateurs.

Next, the climber has to open the metal pole box that the drop lines feed into, and then he must find which line to tap. This takes time, and people are likely to notice. Spies don't like to be noticed.

If the line to be tapped comes from a single-family home, the climber can see where it enters the pole box, but if there is more than one drop wire coming to the pole, such as from an apartment building, finding the right one can be difficult. Usually, all of them go up the outside wall in a group, and

there is no way to tell one from the other.

If the wiretapper knows the number of the line to be tapped and has the telco automatic number identification (ANI), he can use that. When he calls ANI, a computer voice tells him the number he is calling from. If he does not have the ANI number and cannot tell which drop wire is the right one, then there isn't much else he can do.

Once the right line is located, the tapper has two choices: string a wire to someplace where he can set up his listening post, which is not so easy, or install a remote-listen device, an RF transmitter. The obvious choice is the RF bug, taking into consideration size range and battery life.

Sooner or later, the bug will be discovered by the telco maintenance people. Taps have been placed on poles, but not too often.

The telephone company and the police decided that they would decline to prosecute him because of his age, and because they didn't want people to know how easily he had tapped most of the phones on our block. They obviously didn't want anyone to know that a twelve-year-old was an experienced wiretapper.

The above quote came from a true story about tapping telephones in the early fifties.

In a building where the phone lines leave the block through a tube and go directly to the underground conduit, placing a tap is even more difficult. Once underground, the lines soon become part of a larger cable that is often inside a plastic tube that has pressurized nitrogen inside to prevent moisture from affecting the wires.

There are two places the line can be accessed. The first is called a junction point, which is an underground room accessible only from a manhole. Anyone who pulls the cover off in the middle of an intersection (where they usually are located) is likely to be noticed. If the tapper does get in, then he has to find one line out of hundreds, which requires inside telco information.

The other place to access the line is in one of the large metal cabinets located on street corners. These are called bridging or "B" boxes. Even if he does manage to get to the target line, either through a junction point or "B" box, then what is he going to do? A direct-listen method is fine if he wants to set up a listening post there in the underground room, but it could be difficult to string a wire to a remote listening post from the "B" box on a street corner or out of a manhole cover (cars running over the wire and the like). A remote method, an RF transmitter, won't reach very far from inside the metal "B" box or the underground room.

Most down-line taps use one of two methods. First, a long-play recorder with a drop-out relay is hidden in the junction point by someone who can find a place to hide it and access it to switch the tapes and replace the batteries. This is unlikely.

The other option is a bridging tap: connecting the line to be tapped to a second unused line. But there are three requirements for this option to work: there has to be such a second line, that line has to be in a location such that it will be in the same junction point or "B" box as the target line, and then the wiretapper has to find both of them.

Again, this method requires inside information. There are thousands of pairs of wires in these junction points. The wiretapper has to know the specific pair (by its color code) inside a particular binder group to tap. Without inside information, there just is no way.

Down-line taps are very rare, as I said earlier, and are always the work of a pro or telco employee. For example, this is my conception of how the feds would install a court-ordered phone tap. First, they get the court order; then they would contact telco security. Security assigns a special telco employee to the project, and this person determines the location of the target line and selects a junction point to be used. Then they find an unused pair of lines in a cable that goes into the same junction point. This pair is assigned unofficially to the agency making the tap.

(It is also possible that some federal agencies have leased a number of lines for this purpose. If so, they probably have one or more in a number of junctions—if not all.)

The telco employee and the fed go into the junction point and make the bridging tap from the target line to the unused line. The reason for the junction point bridging tap is that if it were done in the telco central office too many people would know about it. A special circuit is used that balances the impedance of the target line so it won't be detected by tap-finding devices.

I also suspect that since the connection is made in the bridging box it wouldn't show up on a TDR. If this is not so, then the telco could arrange for the bridging tap to be placed far enough away from the victim's home or office to prevent the TDR from working. Depending on the type of TDR, one might work from less than few thousand feet (for inexpensive models) to more than two miles (for Tektronix and Hewlett Packard). If the feds believe the quarry is someone who might use a TDR, they will arrange for the tap to beyond its range.

At the feds' offices, probably in a special room for this purpose, the incoming line from the bridging tap would branch off to three open-reel tape recorders. Three are used because the tape might be used as evidence in court, so originals (not copies) have to be made available to the court and the defense attorney.

A question I've been asked: Is it possible to tap my phone if it uses fiberoptic (FO) cable? FO cables don't connect individual phone lines to the telco switching office. They are used as "trunks," large cables that connect one SO to another. FO cables can be tapped, but this is difficult and requires some sophisticated gear and access to the cables.

A FO cable consists of a number of thin strands inside a sheath that would have to be opened from inside a telco junction point or inside the telco office. This is a very big deal. Once the cable sheath is opened, an individual strand could be separated from the rest and bent into a "V" or an "M" shape. Some of the light from the strand will escape from the bends, and this can be detected and amplified with a very specialized and hard-to-get device.

Even then, each strand inside the cable carries a large number of conversations at the same time. This is known as multiplexing: many (conversations) into one (strand). Finding one particular conversation is nearly impossible. Some new lineman's test sets that just became available can tap into fiberoptic cables and communicate with the central office, but they cannot demultiplex (or, find) one particular conversation.

WHAT TO DO WHEN YOU FIND A BUG

If you find a listening device or something you

think might be, first of all, leave it alone for now. Don't say anything to alert the listener that you have found it.

If it is a microphone, make some noise to cover the continued search. If it is an RF transmitter, shield it temporarily with something metal, and never assume that it is the only one. Always assume that there are others.

Look Again

A few years ago I saw a TV movie in which a crook bugged an FBI agent's home (how's that for a switch?) with several devices that included an FM wireless microphone. It was "found" by a neighbor whose FM radio picked up the agent's wife.

So this TV agent reasoned that this was the work of a real pro: using an easy-to-find device as a cover for another one. That's TV. No experienced spy is going to make a listening device easy to find. Even if there are twelve bugs, all will be as difficult to locate as possible, depending on access, what is available, and other variables.

When you are convinced that you have found everything, put things back the way they were and have a pro look over the situation.

Make a Profile

Once you have found a listening device, probably the first things you will want to know are who put it there and why. Generally knowing whom will tell you why. Let's take a look at some ideas on finding the spy.

If it is a battery-powered transmitter, estimate how long it will last. While it is possible for the spy to get in periodically to replace the batteries, this is not usually the case—spies want to get in and out and not come back.

What has happened or is about to happen in the room where it was found, within the time it will still operate? An important meeting? A deposition?

Consider also where it was placed and how long that would take. If the offending device was hidden under a desk using double-sided tape, it could be someone who was in the room only once and who was alone or unwatched for just a few seconds or created a diversion by pretending to drop something or look through an attaché case for some documents.

If, while interviewing someone, you received a call that you left your office to take, consider that the client may have arranged this call to give him or her time to hide the device.

If it was inside of a hollowed-out book that replaced one of yours, this tells you that either the person who placed it was in your office at least twice (once to get one of your seldom-read books and the other time to replace it after the bug was emplaced) or he knew your profession well enough to know that you would you have this book but seldom use it, which means one visit was sufficient.

If it was inside a hollow door, wall plug, light fixture, or other similar hiding place, then whoever placed it had to have access and be left alone for some time. Has there been any remodeling done in the area recently, during which a workman could have installed it? It could be the work of someone who broke into the office or room. If you have security personnel at the doors of your office building and secure locks at home then it was most likely an inside job.

Who could have been alone for the amount of time required to place the device? What do you know about them? Who cleans the offices and empties the wastebaskets? Do you have the carpets steam-cleaned on a regular basis? Who does it? Who of these people would have reason to bug you or might have been paid to install a listening device?

Now consider the degree of sophistication of the device(s). A $20 FM wireless microphone can be purchased by anyone who has twenty bucks. These are of poor quality, compared to the more exotic and expensive types, and, although they do work, they are more likely to be used by someone who has limited knowledge or funds. This is not an absolute, but it is likely.

On the other hand, officers of a well-known religious organization with assets in the hundreds of millions relied on a cheap FM wireless microphone to bug an IRS conference room. They sat in a car outside the building and listened on the radio.

A small bug hidden inside an upholstery button is usually the work of a pro because these devices just aren't that easy to get. The presence of the upholstery bug also means that the installer had to have been in the room at least twice, once to snip a tiny sample of the material to match and once more to install it.

A repeater system, likewise, will be the work of a pro or the government. Getting someone into a window-washing or maintenance crew to place the repeater on the wall of a tall building takes some connections or a bribe.

The use of an obviously homemade bug tells you a little about the person who planted it. It isn't likely to be the feds, and a pro would probably buy rather than build or do a neater job.

If it is built on an etched circuit board that looks sloppy, has traces that are crooked or uneven, or is built on perf board (a thin Bakelite sheet with holes drilled every 1/10 inch), and the solder joints are sloppy, it was probably made by an amateur. The more professional bugs will likely be inside a metal shield so as to be missed by the NLJT.

Consider the probable range of the device, based on output power, antenna size, and where in the room it was placed (if near a window, which one and which direction does it face?).

The power output of the cheaper wireless microphones may be only 10 milliwatts or even less, with a probable range of 100 feet under the best conditions. The range of more expensive units, $50 and up, is about five times as high. This is useful in trying to determine where the listening post is.

Is there a way to trace it? Probably not, but the FBI crime labs are capable of some incredible things. Omnibus is a federal law so the FBI has jurisdiction over its violation. There is a slight chance it could be traced back to whomever installed it. It's worth a try. Put all this information together and see what kind of profile you can build of the person who bugged you.

Make a Plan

Using the profile, decide how to proceed. You can disable the device, feed the listener mislead-ing information, or try to draw him out, either to catch him and try to have him arrested or otherwise dealt with, or to find out who he is and, in turn, bug him.

Deciding how to proceed is dependent upon your situation, but consider feeding the intruder information about something that will be sure to cause him to react. If you say something that causes him to believe that something important is about to take place—a meeting at a location you disclose—the listener may show up to see what he can find out.

The location of such a meeting should be in an area in which it is easy to look for people; the more secluded, esoteric, and important-sounding, the better.

Arrange to have someone get there early and look for known people, write down license numbers, take photographs, etc. See who fits the profile. If one of the license numbers comes back to a carpenter or firm who remodeled your office, a client, or a competitor, you know where to begin your plans.

Destruction of Bugs

Once again, consider whether you want the person who has placed the device to know you have found it before you destroy or disable it. An inside bug can be removed or the battery disconnected. Rather than destroy it, keep it as possible evidence.

If the phone line resistance measurements indicate a bug is attached and you cannot locate it by following the phone line, it can be burned out by sending a burst of low-current high voltage down the line. Burst units are available from some of the suppliers we have listed, and they are very simple to make, but as this involves high voltages and the possibility of damaging the telco lines, I suggest that you have this step done by a professional technician.

PART IV

OUTSIDE DEVICES

Whereas the first three parts of this book were concerned with inside listening devices, part four deals with ways to listen to conversations from a distance without having to enter the area to hide a bug or tap a wire, and one type of microwave bug that is both inside and outside.

Outside listening devices can be active or passive. A shotgun microphone doesn't do anything but listen; it is passive. A laser emits a beam of light; it does something and, thus, is active.

Parabolic Reflectors and Shotgun Microphones

Microphones can be omnidirectional, designed to pick up sound from all directions, or unidirectional, designed to pick up sound from one direction only. However, even unidirectional ones pick up some sound from all directions.

To make a microphone highly directional, it is necessary to place it inside something that narrows or concentrates sound. The first of these is the parabolic reflector, which is much the same as a TV satellite dish on a smaller scale. It can be as small as a few inches across, such as the one made by Tyco as part of its line of Spy-Tech toys (which really works) to a typical hand-held plastic 18-inch model, which works much better than the toy one, to the four-foot tripod-mounted model from CSI.

Sound waves that strike the dish are concentrated and reflected to a focal point where the microphone element is mounted. The problem with parabolic reflectors is that they tend to pick up

sound from the back and are not as able to zero in on someone as the shotgun type.

The shotgun microphone uses one or more long tubes to narrow the area in which it will pick up sound. Neuman makes a shotgun that sells for about $1,200, which is used by broadcasting companies and TV sports reporters, who can afford whatever they want. Another good shotgun mike is made by Sennheiser and sells for about $550.

Shotgun microphones that use more than one tube are sometimes called "Gatling guns" because of their resemblance to the early machine gun. This type of mike was used in the movie *The Manhattan Project*.

A Gatling gun microphone is easy to make. It requires lengths of aluminum or stainless tubing of about 3/8-inch diameter and starting at 1-inch and increasing in 1-inch increments up to 36 inches or so. Bundle these together, with the flush ends covered with a metal or plastic housing that contains the microphone element and is filled with sound-absorbing material. The tubes have to be straight; if slightly bent, they don't conduct the sound as well and can cause distortion.

The performance of any of these directional microphones can be improved by using an equalizer, the same type used in stereo systems. Most microphones will "hear" from about 50 to 20,000 cycles or so; some hear higher, some not as high. The 300 to 3,000 cycle bandwidth used by telephones is more than sufficient. What is missed at the time because of interference can, to some degree, be recovered from a tape recording using the equalizer.

The only way to detect either type is by seeing it, and if the user has it hidden behind acoustically transparent material (e.g., thin curtains or the grille cloth or foam used in speaker systems), it isn't going to be seen.

While outside, not much can be done to avoid being heard by a directional microphone, but at home, neither type can pick up much through closed windows and drapes, and there are only so many places within effective range to hide a four-foot dish or a four-foot Gatling gun.

Although both types work, they cannot zero in on one person in a crowd from a hundred yards away. They can focus on a small group of people from a hundred feet or so, but they cannot pinpoint specific conversations any more reliably than that. And neither mike can hear the spekaer very well if he is facing the opposite direction.

MICROWAVE LISTENING DEVICES

Besides the microwave frequency bugs from an earlier section, there are other ways to use microwaves for surveillance. The first method is to concentrate a microwave beam on something that vibrates from the sound in the room in which it is placed. The reflected beam, coming back, is converted into sound, like the laser devices detailed in the next part.

In the U.S. Embassy in Moscow, the sculpture of the American eagle that the Soviets presented as a gift was made so it would act as a sounding board for reflecting microwaves. Beware of bears bearing gifts. In addition, the steel rebars (reinforcement bars) inside the concrete walls were arranged in such a way that they would also reflect the microwave beam, just like the eagle.

The second method, used both outside and inside, is to plant a small device called a resonator, which looks like several quarter-size metal disks with a small rod through the center, inside the area to be bugged. The resonator may be inside a small metal cylinder. A microwave transmitter is placed somewhere near the target on one side, and a receiver goes on the other side. A concentrated beam from the transmitter is directed at the point where the resonator is hidden.

This device is vibrated by sounds in the room

in which it is placed and modulates the microwave beam. When the receiver picks it up, it can demodulate (recover) this sound. This device is *very* expensive and therefore *very* unlikely to be encountered.

Another system that some scientists in Germany are working on will supposedly reflect the microwave beam from the changing density of the air—sound makes tiny compressions in air, and this system is supposed to convert this change in density into sound.

The principle that this works on is probably similar to one that produces laser holograms. The laser beam is split into two smaller beams. One of them is bounced off a mirror that changes the phase angle, and when the two beams are recombined, they create an image in space. Unlike the lasers in the next part, microwaves penetrate walls and don't require a window. Also, they are unaffected by the things that can interfere with lasers.

FINDING MICROWAVE DEVICES

The operating frequencies of such microwave listening devices can be anywhere in the microwave spectrum, from 3 to 300 gc., but the types that can carry voices are more or less limited to a maximum of 23 gc., which some spectrum analyzers will detect.

All of the microwave engineers I interviewed said that they were not aware of any type of transmitter used for voice transmission above 23 gc. That area is used for telemetry, radar, deep space exploration, and satellites, and the transmissions are nonvoice: pulse code modulation, multiplexed signals, and so forth.

The chances of such a system being used on you are slim. They are very expensive and require skilled people to set them up and operate them; they are primarily used by the federal government. Unless you are very important to them, there is little chance of their using this against you.

Special microwave receivers are available that tune the area, such as one made by Condor Systems in Silicon Valley. The spectrum analyzer will also detect microwave transmissions.

The names of other manufacturers of microwave surveillance receivers are in the list of suppliers in Appendix C.

LASERS: HOW THEY WORK

This method of eavesdropping was allegedly devised by CIA. A laser and a telescope are mounted on a tripod, and the laser beam is pointed at a target window. Part of the light beam passes through the glass, and part is reflected back to the telescope.

This reflected beam is "seen" by the telescope, and the light from the eyepiece is focused on a photocell that turns variations in the light into electrical impulses. These are converted into sound and amplified so the listener can hear it.

The target windows vibrate slightly from the sound inside the room, and this tiny difference in the distance from the laser to the window produces the variations in light that are recovered as sound. It is just that simple—in theory.

The laser has to be placed so that the target reflects the beam exactly back to the telescope. If the angle is not very precise, the reflected beam will miss it. Theoretically and under ideal conditions, it can hear clearly what is being said in the target room from miles away, but many things can interfere with reception. Dust, fog, rain, street noise, passing aircraft, vibrations in the target building (including elevators, heavy equipment in the basement, anything that can interfere with the beam or cause the window to vibrate) all considerably reduce the effectiveness of the laser listening device. Good-quality audio-filtering equipment can improve the system somewhat, as can using a different type of laser, but it is still far from perfect.

The obvious reason for using a laser for surveillance is that no penetration (entering the target area to install a listening device) is required; the listener doesn't have to go anywhere near the target.

Because lasers don't work that well most of the time, practitioners have devised a way to improve this method that requires the spy to get close to but not inside the target. A small contact microphone is placed in the corner of a window where it is least likely to be seen. A thin wire is used to lead to an audio amplifier hidden nearby, which, depending on the amount of space available, has a large long-lasting battery. Then the audio from the amplifier goes to a speaker that is mounted on a thin glass plate. This is placed inside a specially made case that absorbs vibrations that would interfere with reception. The laser is focused on the glass plate, which the speaker causes to vibrate, just like the windows, and is reflected back the same way. This improves reception considerably and can still be used from a long distance.

A semitechnical explanation of lasers might be useful here. Laser stands for "light amplification by stimulated emission of radiation." The principle of a laser is quite simple. The original ruby laser consisted of a small rod made of synthetic ruby (aluminum oxide and chromium) about 1 centimeter (cm.) in diameter and 10 cm. long, which is polished and mirrored on the ends, and a high-intensity light source such as a camera electronic flash unit, which is placed close to the rod. When the light flashes, some of the light enters the rod (which is called an optical resonator) from the sides. Some of the light strikes the mirrored ends and is reflected to the opposite end and then bounces back and forth. As it does this, it strikes some of the chromium atoms and causes them to emit more light particles (photons), and this process (amplification) continues until the intensity of the light is so great that the mirror on one end (which is slightly less reflective) cannot contain it, and it bursts out in a flash of red light.

Since the mirrored ends are nearly perfectly parallel, the beam is likewise parallel; it stays focused and does not spread out like other types of light.

Lasers can be made from a variety of materials such as glass tubes filled with various gases (helium, neon, carbon dioxide), liquids, or solids. They have even been made from Jell-O and vodka.

A laser that can change wavelengths is the "tuned dye" type. The lasing medium is a liquid that flows through the resonator, and as the color changes, the wavelength changes. These are expensive and usually are confined to laboratories, but they are being developed as a surveillance laser, to compensate for fog and dust, etc.

A laser that will work as a listening device can be purchased at surplus electronics stores for about a hundred dollars, but at that price it will be a helium-neon laser, the type used in supermarket check-out stands. It produces a bright red beam. If you point it at a window, someone will see it.

Invisible infrared lasers start at about $750 and are available from Edmund Scientific Company.

These are all low-power lasers; their output is a few thousandths of one watt. The types used by government agencies to spy are much higher in power, one watt or more. These types are very dangerous. If a person were to be hit square in the eye by such a laser, to quote an engineer from a company that makes them, "The first thing you would notice would be your eyeball exploding."

The telescope need not be anything fancy; a small, inexpensive Tasco, often found in pawn shops for less than a hundred dollars, works fine. The electronics are also not complicated: the IR receiver described elsewhere will work, and it is another device that any technician can build.

Before you go out and buy a laser to try this system, read a few books on lasers and safety, and keep in mind that when you point one of these concentrated light devices at someone, there is a good chance of causing eye damage.

FINDING LASERS

"If it can see you, then you can see it."

Kodak IR Detection Products and Sunstone IR converters are card-size devices that are charged by exposing them to normal visible light. Once charged, they will glow when exposed to infrared light. These devices are also available from Edmund Scientific Company.

The TD-53 bug detector that will find the IR bugs mentioned above will also locate a laser beam. Since the laser beam has to strike the target window at a precise 90-degree angle for it to work, it obviously has to come from a location that is at the same height as and in a direct line to the target, so it's not very difficult to pinpoint the source.

DEFEATING LASERS

The easiest way to prevent being listened to by a laser is to tape a small transistor radio to your windows. Tune it to a rock station and send the listener some good vibrations.

Naturally, this will alert your listener that you are protecting yourself, which you may not want to do. In that case, heavy drapes will make the laser useless, as will an air conditioner in the window or anything that causes the glass to vibrate. The "cone of silence" used by Maxwell Smart on "Get Smart" will also work. This is a little extreme for most people, but something similar was used in the U.S. Embassy in Moscow.

PART V

COMPUTER EAVESDROPPING

You are a psychiatrist who has just finished a session with one of your patients, and you are using your personal computer to transcribe and print your notes for the file. The patient is an electronics engineer who works for a company that makes nuclear weapons. He is psychologically incapable of having a "normal" sexual relationship, and the only outlet he has for his repressed desires comes from watching others doing what he cannot. He is a voyeur, a Peeping Tom.

A surveillance van is parked on the street several blocks away, and inside it is a modified TV set whose screen displays every word you type. Later, foreign agents follow your patient, watching and videotaping him through sophisticated night-viewing equipment. Then they confront and blackmail him into revealing classified information.

Like most people who have computers, you had no way of knowing that this is possible. There were no warning labels on the case or in the manuals, and the dealer didn't tell you because he didn't know.

TEMPEST AND VAN ECK TECHNOLOGY

We called twenty computer stores and talked to the sales people about van Eck and TEMPEST. Not even one of them had ever heard of it. TEMPEST is an acronym for Transient Electromagnetic Pulse Emanation Standard, which concerns the amount of electromagnetic radiation that is generated by computer terminals and monitors and the levels that are considered safe from eavesdropping by the van Eck system. These safe levels, or "standards," are detailed in technical report NACSIM 5100A, which has been classified by the National Security Agency.

More technical stuff: whenever an electric current changes in voltage level, it generates electromagnetic pulses that radiate into space like radio waves. In a computer monitor, as in a television set, an electron gun sends out a beam of electrons (electric current), and when these electrons strike the screen, they cause the coating on the screen to glow. This beam scans across the screen in a series of lines, from top to bottom, and "paints" the picture one line at a time.

As the electron beam scans, it flashes off and on to make the screen light and dark, and these changes in the voltage level generate the signal that the van Eck system receives. The base frequencies most monitors "transmit" on are from 50 to 75 mc., but they also have harmonics, multiples of the base frequency. For example, the EVGA monitor used with this system transmits a strong signal on 61.31 and 63.495, and the seventh harmonics are fairly strong in the 428 to 430 mc. area. If you have a personal computer and a scanner that receives this area, set it to search 52 to 74, and you will hear your monitor as a loud buzzing sound that changes whenever you punch a key. The range of 54 to 72 mc. is TV VHF channels 2, 3, and 4.

Why, you ask, don't I pick up my monitor on my TV set? The internal signals in monitors are different from those in television sets. To convert a TV so that it will receive a monitor, one must generate these signals and inject them into the TV as "composite sync" or synchronization.

The system that does this is known as the van Eck technology, which is the result of research done by Dr. Wim van Eck at the Neher Laboratories in Holland. He conducted a demonstration of his new system, which is detailed in publications listed in Appendix I.

The van Eck device is not especially complicated. Any electronics engineer can design it, and anyone familiar with digital electronics can build it. It consists only of a small circuit board, a dozen integrated circuits, and a few other components, all available at commercial electronics or surplus stores.

The device is usually built into a small black and white TV with a very directional antenna connected to it, and it can receive a monitor from half a mile away or so. The TV screen will display whatever is on the target computer, and it can be stored on videotape.

A schematic diagram of the van Eck snooping device is available from Consumertronics.

DEFEATING VAN ECK

I do not know if using van Eck technology is legal or not. Omnibus prohibits "intercepting a wire communication," which computer data is not.

Omnibus also makes illegal the use of any "electronic, mechanical, or other device to intercept any oral communication," which computer data is not.

Possibly, it would cover interception of data if the computer were connected to another computer by phone line, because it would be intercepting a wire communication that is part of an interstate wire system, the phone lines.

Anyone with the funds and the desire can set up a van Eck system in a van and roam around to see what he can find, and there is no way to detect them with electronic equipment.

Since there are people who can monitor your monitor, start by not using your system to process anything sensitive, if you can avoid it, until the system is secured. If you transfer data over the phone lines, encrypt it.

SECURING METHODS

The government spy agencies have many of their computers located in underground rooms, where they are secure from van Eck systems.

Those that are above ground are often inside vaults, as in the book and movie *The Falcon and the Snowman.* These are Faraday cages, which have heavy copper-mesh shielding that prevents radiation leakage.

Such methods are a little extreme for the average person or small business, but Wang manufactures computer systems that are secured against the van Eck eavesdropping method. A Wang VGA 386 system sells for about $5,000, compared to an IBM-clone 386, available for $2,000 or so at many computer stores. But this is a small price to pay for secure data.

Wang's TEMPEST secure systems do more than just shield the computer to stop it from transmitting; they are designed and built in a different way. That's all Wang would tell me. To buy one, you have to "show some ID" and sign statements about not exporting it to a foreign country. National security . . .

If the Wang is too expensive or doesn't fit your needs, you can make your system less susceptible to van Eck eavesdropping. TEMPEST radiation comes mainly from the monitor but can also be detected from the other parts of the system: keyboard, cables, printer, and the motherboard.

The monitor can be shielded by placing it in a metal housing. A 16-gauge metal box made by a sheet metal shop that is grounded provides a good start. All cables should be shielded (some already are, but ribbon cables are not) and grounded, and the metal computer case should also be grounded.

Once this is done, use a scanner to see if you still hear it. Move the scanner farther away and try it again. Now check the harmonics.

A good scanner has a sensitivity (in the VHF and UHF bands) of one microvolt or less. If the scanner cannot hear the monitor across the room, then a van Eck device isn't likely to hear it from across the street.

Having two monitors of the same type operating in the same area may confuse a van Eck system. Use a scanner to check both of them to see if they are transmitting on the same frequency. If so, then keep both running at the same time.

Keeping the brightness up and the contrast down slightly reduces the strength of the TEMPEST radiation, and anything metal between the monitor and the outside walls, such as filing cabinets, also helps.

Elenco Electronics has a TV jammer that transmits a signal on the same frequencies as a monitor. It comes in kit form, has less than a dozen parts (including a premade circuit board) and instructions, and costs just $6. This is another project that electronics students often build as a lab exercise. They could easily add a one-transistor amplifier to increase the power, which should jam a van Eck listener very effectively.

COMPUTER DATA ENCRYPTION

It wasn't that many years ago that computers were available only to the government and big businesses, and only they could encrypt data to keep it secret. Then, in the seventies, this changed. The Apple II and IBM PC hit the market, and almost anyone could afford to buy a computer.

Suddenly, massive amounts of information were being stored in very small places and being transferred through the phone lines all over the world. This placed such information at great risk, as it is a little easier to steal a floppy disk or two than a filing cabinet, and tapping phones isn't terribly difficult. A way to keep confidential information confidential had to be found.

A number of old "pencil and paper" encryption schemes were quickly rewritten into computer programs, and now anyone who had a computer could encrypt information and keep it private—something that certain government agencies didn't like very much.

There are a number of these programs, that provide varying degrees of security, from modest to literally unbreakable, and costing from nothing to several hundred dollars. The two most important, and secure, programs are the RSA and the DES.

THE RSA PUBLIC KEY SYSTEM

The problem with most encryption systems is not that someone will be able to crack them; it is key distribution. In a business or government agency, there are certain people who have to have the key to access to confidential data, and there is always the chance that, as it is passed from one authorized person to another, it might fall into the hands of someone who is not authorized to have it—such as a spy.

The answer to this problem is the public key system. The public key system uses two keys or passwords. One is the public key, which can be made available to anyone, and the other is the private key, which the person using the program keeps secret. Having someone's public key does not weaken the system or make it possible to derive the private key.

If someone wants to send a secret message to someone else, he uses that person's public key to encrypt it and then send it to him. Only the recipient can unscramble it by using his private key, so the problem of key distribution is eliminated.

THE DATA ENCRYPTION STANDARD

The Data Encryption Standard (DES; Project Lucifer) was developed in 1977 by IBM for the National Bureau of Standards (now the National Institute of Standards and Technology, or NIST) and the National Security Agency and is still a formidable method of encrypting data.

As originally written, it encrypted data in 64-bit (8-byte) blocks, but this was later changed to 56 bits—the government wanted a program that only it could break with its multimillion-dollar supercomputers, but 64 bits was too difficult for even federal agencies. These 56 bits of text can be arranged in any of 2 ^ 56 possible combinations, which is 7.2 x 10 ^ 16 or 72,057,000,000,000,000.

DES PROGRAMS

The Private Line DES

The Private Line (version 6.0, April 1988) is available from Everett Enterprises of Springfield, Virginia, for approximately $49.99. It is menu-driven and very easy to use as no knowledge of programming is required. Just follow the instructions.

It allows the user to quickly switch DES modes[1] from ECB to CFB to CBC, the documentation is well written, it also has the secure-erase[2] feature, and the user can select the number of passes. TPL allows the user to "double encrypt" file, using two different keys, which greatly increases security.

Some other nice things TPL has: it will output the file in ASCII for transmission over phone lines or LANs; you can view the file in HEX; it has a print option; and it has a built-in routine that performs the 171 tests that are required to ensure that it is in compliance with the original DES algorithm.

SUPER CRYPT DES

"Super-Crypt" (version 3.0, December 1990) is available from Super Software for around $59 plus postage. Super Crypt is also menu-driven (has nice pull-down menus) and is also very easy to use—just follow the instructions.

When you open the program, it prompts you for the subdirectory of the file(s) to be encrypted, which then appears on the screen.

Then you can select multiple files to encrypt and which of the two levels of security you wish to use. The program even tells you how long it will take. Both of these are very nice features.

It also has secure erase (the user can select the number of passes) and has the option of automatically deleting and secure-erasing plain-text files after they have been encrypted.

PUBLIC KEY PROGRAMS

MailSafe

The public key program "MailSafe" is available

from RSA Data Security, Inc. for approximately $125. MailSafe is menu-driven and is the easiest of the public key programs to use. Generating the two (public and private) keys is done by simply following the prompts on the screen.

Once this is done, the main menu is accessed, the desired operation is selected, and the file to be encrypted or decrypted is easily called up by moving the light bar and hitting the enter key.

MailSafe not only encrypts messages, it has other features that make sending data even more secure. Two of these are the "digital envelope" and the "digital signature."

The MailSafe Digital Envelope

Suppose Alice decides to send a secret message to Bob. First, she encrypts the message with the DES, using a random key, and then she finds Bob's public key, and uses it to encrypt the DES key. The encrypted document and encrypted DES key are combined to form the "digital envelope" and sent to Bob. Only Bob can decrypt it, using his private key, to get the DES key, which is then used to decrypt the original message.

The MailSafe Digital Signature

Now to create a "digital signature" (which will authenticate the sender): Alice runs her document through a "hashing algorithm," which produces a "message digest," which is unique to each document. Then she uses her private key to encrypt the message digest, which produces the "digital signature" and sends it along with the document to Bob. When Bob receives this, he uses the same hashing algorithm to create a new message digest and also decodes Alice's message digest using her public key. Then the two message digests are compared. If they are identical, then the digital signature is authentic and has not been tampered with.

RSA works both ways. If a message is encrypted with someone's public key, it can be decrypted only with that person's private key, or if that person uses his private key to encrypt the message, then only his public key can decrypt it.

THE IRIS PUBLIC KEY PROGRAM

IRIS is a shareware RSA program that can be

downloaded from some computer bulletin boards. It also has the DES and several other encryption programs such as Bazeries, Playfair, and Enigma₁.

The present version of IRIS is not menu-driven, but a new soon-to-be-released version will be. It is produced in England, and using it in the United States requires a license from RSA Data Security, Inc.

HOW SECURE ARE THESE PROGRAMS?

The Data Encryption Standard

The world's fastest computer, the thirty-million-dollar Cray YMP supercomputer, can make more than two billion "flips," floating point instructions per second. If each of these calculations could try one of the possible DES combinations, it would take about 417 days to try them all. If the information was double encrypted, it would take years. The government would have to be very interested in the information to tie up one of its (many) Crays for that long. It has better things to do with its time, such as spying on library patrons and antiwar demonstrators.

For years there have been rumors circulating in the intelligence community and on computer bulletin boards and networks that the DES has "been broken"—that it has a "trap door," a secret way of breaking the code, that only the government knows about. When you consider that the DES was written FOR the government, I wouldn't be at all surprised (the feds are not above such trickery), but the source code for the DES has been available for years and has been examined, tested, and taken apart by dozens of expert programmers. If this were true, the world would know about it.

The RSA Public Key System

The RSA public key system is the most secure encryption system that is available to "we the people."[3]

First of all, RSA can use a longer key. The DES key is only 56 bits long, but the key length of the RSA algorithm is almost unlimited. A 250-digit key length would make for more than $10 \wedge 200$ possible ways to arrange a block of text. Numbers with exponents that big are beyond comprehension to all but mathmeticians and the Treasury Department.

The Cray YMP would be able to break the 200-digit key in about two million years. Maybe. If key distribution is not a problem, then the DES is secure

enough, but if you are in a situation in which the key has to be made available to a number of people, then obviously a public key program is indicated.

Keep in mind that if you use the RSA or DES to encrypt something, you must not lose the key. If you do, your data is gone forever. There is nothing anyone can do to get it back.

THE PAK-RAT EXPERIMENT

I would like to hear from anyone who has tried the following experiment, which I conducted last year (write to the author in care of Paladin Press, P.O. Box 1307, Boulder, CO 80306). I used an AT (286) computer with a clock speed of 10 mc. and a Casper TTL amber monitor, a high-frequency receiver, a Toshiba portable computer, and a Pak-Rat II decoder.

I started a program that converts text on the screen to Morse code, and while the speaker was beeping out the listings of the hard-disk directory, I tuned the receiver to a number of frequencies from 442 kc. to 20 mc. (A scanner that covers 50 to 75 mc. was not available at the time). With the receiver feeding into the decoder and the Toshiba, it printed on its screen the same information that was on the screen of the AT.

I moved the receiving equipment to a motor home parked in front of the house and set it up to run on the generator. By using a small whip antenna, I got the same result. I don't know which of the many signals in the computer I was receiving or if it was a subharmonic of the monitor, but it did work.

The decoder is too slow to work with a normal program running on the main system, but if a much faster ASCII decoder were available, it might work. This would be an improvement on the van Eck method as the received information could be stored on disk and would not require the use of a VCR.

TYPEWRITERS

Some electronic typewriters also generate electronic pulses that can be detected and converted to reveal what is being typed. They should be shielded and grounded to protect sensitive data that you don't want others getting their hands on.

IBM Selectric typewriters, which are not elec-

tronic, have to be modified internally to radiate a signal—or so I have been led to believe.

¹ These programs will be detailed in my next book, which will have a long and comprehensive chapter on encryption, computer hacking, and security.

² Secure-erase writes over the old plain-text file so it can never be recovered.

³ A number of big companies such as Novell, DEC, Lotus Development Corporation, Motorola, and Microsoft use MailSafe. These places have umpteen software engineers and programmers per square foot, many of whom would have checked it out thoroughly before trusting it. If there were a "trap door" in MailSafe, they would have found it long ago, and RSA Data Security, Inc. would be long gone.

PART VI

VIDEO OPTICAL SURVEILLANCE

A person can be under video surveillance at work, on the street, in a car, anywhere he or she goes. Retail stores, banks, airports, parking lots, shopping centers, and drive-up windows all have video cameras. The lenses inside cars or vans can be disguised as reflectors or mirrors or as specially made periscopes that look like air vents. People can even be under video surveillance in their homes and offices and not know it.

Pinhole lenses that allow surveillance through 1/8-inch holes can be disguised as sprinklers, and very thin fiberoptic probes can peek through keyholes, under doors, through the openings in wall plug covers from adjoining offices, light fixtures from upstairs apartments, or through other small openings. Or an opening can be made.

A forgotten briefcase can contain a camera that will transmit to a neighbor's house, a nearby apartment, or a van parked on the street.

AVAILABLE EQUIPMENT

The latest thing in video surveillance is a very small, self-contained camera and transmitter from Interphase. It is 2.8 x 1.6 x 5.6 inches. The 100-milliwatt transmitter will send the signal 100 feet or more, depending on conditions. Fascinating.

Infrared night-viewing devices allow surveillance in total darkness by emitting a beam of IR light, and starlight scopes use ambient starlight amplified by a photomultiplier tube or other device to "see" inside dark rooms if the curtains are open. Edmund Scientific and Sherwood offer such night-viewing devices.

DEFEATING VIDEO SURVEILLANCE

Inside video surveillance is not difficult or expensive to prevent. The easiest way is to repaint around any place where there could be a small opening, such as ceiling light fixtures, and plug the wall outlets as with the tube microphones in Part I.

A careful physical search will uncover a hidden camera or the lens, and there are video camera detectors that pick up the signals that cameras generate. Capri has one that uses a directional antenna.

Fiberoptic probes are flexible and can be worked through small holes behind cabinets, bookshelves, or other furniture if the person using them knows the layout of the target room. What (and who) is on the other side of your walls?

Check air vents and hot air registers, both favorite hiding places. If you find a pinhole lens opening, you can simply cover it with tape, or you can buy a laser that will disable the camera it is connected to at electronics surplus stores for less than $100. Poetic justice, I think.

Keep blinds and drapes closed, place a felt strip on the bottom of doors, and block any opening through which a lens can look, and no one will be able to use video devices against you.

Should you find a camera, you can disable it or leave it in place and feed it misleading information to draw out the person who placed it. Even though pinhole lenses can see through such small holes, the rest of the equipment is much larger. In a home, there aren't many places to hide it and to do so requires access and time, which make it more unlikely.

Video equipment is also expensive. Surveillance cameras alone run $300 to $1,000; a pinhole lens costs several hundred; a transmitter to send the signal can cost $2,000, plus a monitor and VCR. It gets rather spendy.

Those who can afford to install such equipment realize that the victim might find it, so they have to accept the loss. You find it, you own it.

There is absolutely no reason anyone should have to be under video surveillance in his or her own home.

TWO-WAY TELEVISION?

People have asked me if it is true that a TV set can "see" the people who are watching it. A TV, as with many other things, can have a small video camera hidden inside it.

But can a TV set, as it is manufactured, watch you? Is this some secret way for the government to spy on you? The answer is no. I spent three unexciting terms in college studying the boob tube, and I know what is inside them.

What about a cable TV converter box? Yes, a video camera could possibly be hidden inside your converter, but it isn't likely. First of all, there isn't enough space in most of them. Even if there were, it would take hours to install a camera, which means someone would have to have that much time in your home or office or be able to switch yours with one that has a camera.

The spy would have to know the type you have (there are many to choose from) and then duplicate any identifying marks on your converter that you are used to seeing. He would also have to be able to program the converter for the same premium channels. If he did not do so, when you turned to HBO to watch a movie and found no HBO, you'd call the cable company and raise hell. The customer service representative would tell you that your HBO *was* on, the next day you'd return the converter and get another one, and the spy would be out several thousand bucks.

The last drawback to using a cable box to spy on you is the fact that such a camera has a range of no more than a few hundred feet, which limits the area available for a listening post.

It isn't likely that someone would choose to watch you from the cable converter, but it is possible. If someone did bug your cable, there is a nifty way to defeat it. The Powermid system from the Heath Company is basically a device for using an infrared remote control to control something in another room. It relays the signal from the remote control. Hide the cable converter behind the TV set where it can't see anything and use the Powermid. If you are the feisty type, tape a few hours of commercials, point the converter at your TV, and play them back.

Another way to defeat the spy's setup is to set the converter so it points at a wall and place a small mirror on that wall. Bounce the beam from your remote control off the mirror so the cable box will still work.

Could the camera send a signal through the cable to the cable company, or to someplace where a spy has tapped into it? Yes, it could. Cable TV companies can send many channels through one wire because each channel has a different frequency.

A spy (a very high-tech spy) could modify the camera's transmitter to work on an unused frequency and watch it on his own set with a modified converter, but the cable company would prob-

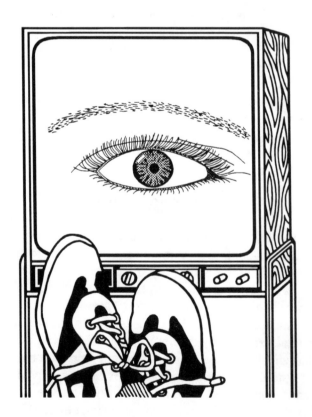

ably notice this very quickly. Then it would send someone around to find out what was going on and ask some rather hard-to-answer questions.

As far as the cable company using converter boxes to spy on customers, it's not likely. It would have to arrange for you to get one of the converters with a camera in it, either by having someone break in and switch boxes or by having someone come to your home and tell you that the one you have has been "recalled by the factory" or some such story. If two unsmiling cable employees wearing suits show up at your door with a new converter, be suspicious.

Seriously, if cable companies began to use such an insidious method of spying, they wouldn't be able to keep it secret for long, and when people found out, the loss of subscribers would put them out of business. No one is that addicted to The Disney Channel.

Finally, there is the cost. Who is going to go to all this trouble and expense just to watch you watching the tube? It's too much money for something that is so hard to install and easy to defeat.

What about audio surveillance through the cable system? This is easier and much cheaper than video and certainly possible, but, again, it is farfetched. The same factors that make it impractical for an individual to watch you through the converter apply to his listening to you. And if a cable company is not willing to risk watching you, it's not going to listen in. But just in case, if a microphone were used in the system, it could be defeated by blocking all the openings in the case. You can also take it apart and look.

Since the converter is usually placed on top of the TV, the sound from the speaker would partially block what it was trying to hear so the microphone could be hidden in the remote control. Again, take it apart and see. Or install a small slide switch to turn the battery off when you aren't using it.

I seriously doubt that cable TV is being used for surveillance, but one way to be 100 percent sure is to kick the TV habit. Rent videos or, better yet, get a library card. They're free.

PART VII

OTHER SURVEILLANCE METHODS

Believe it or not, there are even more ways for those who wish to know your business to spy on you. These include monitoring your mail, ultraviolet-sensitive chemicals that leave behind evidence of your presence wherever you go, bumper beepers, and electronic trackers.

RAIN, SLEET, AND GLOOM OF NIGHT

Your mail can be opened and resealed without your knowing it, using the techniques in the book, *CIA Flaps and Seals Manual* (available from Paladin Press). This book details methods of dry opening, steam opening, and resealing; using two knitting needles to wrap the contents in a tight spiral and then slipping them through the corners of the envelope where there is no glue; avoiding covert traps set by the sender; and much more. The book also has some good information on defeating these methods and makes for some interesting reading.

Opening a person's mail is illegal without a court order, but there are other methods spies can use. They can have the post office make copies of the front of the envelopes that you send and receive. There is no law against this, and as the saying goes, even though this might not tell someone what is inside an envelope, sometimes it's enough to know who is communicating with whom. If the government, or a spy who is paying off a postal worker, were investigating you, having the names of people with whom you are corresponding could open up a whole new approach.

Another trick is to spray a sealed envelope with

Freon that makes the envelope transparent so the user can see some of what is inside. It disappears without a trace, much like the user.

Spray cans of Freon are often resold with different labels such as "secret formula letter bomb detection fluid," "X-Ray Spray," and so forth at a substantial markup—often in the $20 to $30 range. A 16-ounce can of Freon is available from Jameco for $8.95 and can also be found in some electronics supply houses; it is used for cleaning parts.

Using envelopes with a black pattern on the inside prevents this method from working, as will wrapping the envelope's contents in dark paper.

If you believe someone is tampering with your mail, arrange to have anything sensitive sent to you under a different name, in care of a friend or business associate. You can have letters mailed from a different city by placing them without a return address in a larger envelope and sending it to the postmaster in that city. If it is addressed and has the right postage, the post office has to try to deliver it.

I tried this by mailing five letters to five different cities, and I received all five. Four of them were postmarked in the place to which I sent them, but the post office apparently sent one back to the city from where I mailed it; it had the local postmark.

Also, consider computer bulletin boards. There are thousands of them all over America, and many are linked together in networks. Some of these permit encrypted messages. Compuserve, for example one of the largest and most expensive, has no restrictions on this. The "Fido" net forwards electronic mail all over the world and is usually free.

STICKY FINGERS

There are a number of chemicals that "glow" under ultraviolet light, such as calcium silicate, which produces an orange light, and zinc orthosilicate, which glows greenish yellow.

Mixed into a solution, they can be painted on any surface and will stick to the fingers of anyone who touches it and then rub off on whatever that person touches.

Businesses use them to see where their employees go when the boss isn't around, and in Moscow, the Soviets painted the stuff on doorknobs to follow U.S. Embassy staff.

These substances are available from places such as The Spy Factory and The Intelligence Group, or chemical supply houses. Anyone can buy them, and anyone can use them to "follow" you wherever you go.

BUMPER BEEPERS, LOJACK, AND CATS

The "bumper beeper" is a small RF transmitter that can be hidden anywhere on a motor vehicle. The name comes from the method of attaching it to the vehicle—a small magnet is attached to the transmitter, which adheres to the bumper.

The device emits a beep that is picked up by a "chase" vehicle. It has a special receiver with a rotating antenna to tell which direction the beep signal is coming from and a meter to measure the signal's strength. This device does not pick up voices, it only transmits the beep.

Lojack is a system for tracking stolen cars that was originally set up in the east, and is now installed in Massachusetts, Michigan, New Jersey, Florida, Illinois, and Los Angeles County.

For $595, the Lojack company will install a special type of transmitter in your car. Then, should it be stolen, the local police or the FBI can turn the transmitter on by remote control and track wherever it goes. This is a great idea for recovering stolen cars, but it could also be used by law enforcement to track anyone that has it. The Lojack system transmits on 908.000 mc.

A bug can be placed inside a car, just as anywhere else. One clever method someone thought of was to place the bug and a large battery in a stuffed toy tiger that gas stations used to give away.

It could be quickly switched, and you probably would never know.

A bug hidden under the dash or rear deck would probably never be found and is easily wired to the electrical system. Since there is so much space available, it would even be possible to wire in a special circuit, including a transmit/receive (TR) switch and a sound-activated relay. If the car's radio or stereo system is not being used, the sound-activated relay will sense this and trigger the TR switch to connect the car's antenna to the bug to increase its range.

A bug could be hidden inside a dummy turn signal flasher, the dome light, a mirror, a sun visor—the possibilities are almost endless.

Like any other bug, it has to have an antenna of some kind, and this is especially true in a vehicle because the steel body shields the signal. Look for a wire with one end that is not connected to anything. Inside the trim around doors is a likely place for an antenna wire. A good automotive electrician can find wires that shouldn't be there.

1984

The following is considered by some as an "opportunity" for some people to remain free when they otherwise would be locked up. If the general theme of this book—freedom and personal privacy—has made itself manifest, then the reader can guess that I do not agree. It's like burning books—once it starts, where does it end?

A few years ago, an electronic tracking device was developed that worked with the telephone system. A small transmitter was built with an ankle or wrist strap attached that would register on the receiver connected to the phone when it was within range.

The purpose was to keep track of parolees, to tell if they were home when they were supposed to be. Use of this device was "voluntary." The prisoner either volunteered or stayed in prison. The strap was attached to the convict in such a way that if it was removed, an alarm would alert the parole authorities and police. This wasn't good enough for the keepers, and so a number of "improvements" have been made in this system.

Today, a person arrested on suspicion of a crime can be forced into the same deal as a convicted felon, i.e., "volunteer" to wear the tracking device or stay in jail for a year or so until the trial. This is part of the federal government's pretrial services system.

These "improvements" include electronic voice verification, a Breathalyzer to detect consumption of any alcohol, and a camera that can photograph the person wearing the device in his or her own home.

One day soon, anyone the government "thinks might commit a crime" might be forced into the same situation.

1984 is getting close . . .

PART VIII

PREVENTING SURVEILLANCE

Once an area has been made clean, there are many things you can do to help keep it that way. You must first consider how likely you are to be bugged and by whom? If you are not involved in any criminal activities such as drug dealing and are not a political activist who openly criticizes the present administration, then you aren't likely to be bugged by Big Brother. They don't have the manpower to bug everyone, and you probably don't have anything to say that they care about.

If you are not a person who has confidential company information—such as trade secrets or formulas or designs for a new product—or an attorney working on a big case, then big business has little reason to bug you.

No matter who or what you are or aren't, there is the possibility that someone who has become mad at you for some reason, either real or imagined, or has picked you at random because he or she had the opportunity, will bug you. Such persons are usually amateurs who use unsophisticated and inexpensive listening devices.

Your next consideration is how far are you willing to go to prevent being bugged?

SECURING THE AREA

The first step is to protect your property from spies the same way you would from any other intruders. Even if you aren't concerned about being bugged, the increasing number of burglaries is a good reason to do this.

A number of excellent books are available from Paladin on the subjects of burglary, breaking and entering, and lock picking that will tell you a great deal about how it is done and how to keep it from happening to you.

Start with secure locks. It has been said that locks do little more than to keep honest people honest. There is a lot of truth to this. There are dozens of brands of locks on the market, some of which can be opened with ordinary picks. While researching this manual, I read a few books on the subject of picking locks and then found a professional locksmith who agreed to let me try it.

In his shop, he let me use a set of picks and a very popular brand of lock. On my first try at picking, I had it open in less than five minutes. I was impressed. He was not. He already knew how easy it is to pick some locks.

A much more effective device is the Cobra electric lock pick, which slightly resembles an electric toothbrush. It has a pick that is inserted into the lock, and when it is turned on, it vibrates the pins inside the lock up and down and a tension tool turns the core. It will open many locks in seconds—probably the one on your front door.

A set of lockpicks costs less than $20. The Cobra sells for about $225. Both are illegal to possess in most states but are available to anyone who has the money and is determined to get them.

The Cobra will not open an Abloy lock. Nor will anything else except the key. It is pickproof but expensive.

Some locks and some keys have a code number stamped on them. This number is used by a locksmith to make duplicates, which they will for anyone who has it. If any of your keys have numbers on them, have new ones made. Also look on the bottom of Master brand padlocks to make sure the code stenciled on the bottom has been scratched off.

Some doors can be opened by removing the hinge pins. This is easily prevented. There are special screws that can be used to replace the ones in the hinges, and they only cost a few dollars. Locksmiths and hardware stores have them.

The windows in the average home are often the weakest link. While metal-frame casement windows are very secure—they can't be opened from the outside without breaking the glass—the locks on double-hung windows are easily defeated.

The swing lock made by Belwith is available at any hardware store for less than $2. It is made for doors that open inward but can be installed on double-hung windows in five minutes and will prevent them from being opened from the outside.

Drilling a small hole at a downward angle in the window frames is another good method. The hole needs to go through the frame of the top half of the window and partway into the bottom one. Then place a nail in the hole, and it won't slide open.

Wrought-iron bars keep intruders out. Sliding glass doors are easily opened but can be secured with a dowel placed in the bottom of the track.

A PRISONER IN YOUR OWN HOME?

Alarm systems are good for scaring away some burglars, but an experienced spy knows that ringing alarm bells are often ignored for long periods of time. They can often break in, make the drop (plant a listening device), and disappear long before anyone comes around to investigate. We have all heard alarms ringing in a downtown or residential area without seeing anyone responding to them. It is far better to keep anyone from getting in than to depend on an alarm system to scare them away.

At home, one of the best deterrents is man's best friend, the dog. An aggressive German shepherd or Doberman that prefers spies to Alpo will give a would-be intruder second thoughts.

If someone does get in to hide a bug, a voice-activated tape recorder can be used to capture the sounds he made, which will tell you what he was up to. A hidden video camera is even better.

The Heath Company has a video surveillance camera for $300 and a video transmitter that will relay the signal to a VCR nearby for another $100.

You can also make it hard for an intruder to find a place to hide a listening device. Anything that can be opened and could hide a bug, as detailed in previous chapters, can be secured by painting over the screws with invisible solutions of the chemicals mentioned above that glow under UV light. Plastic covers on VCRs, switch boxes, phones, the backs of TV sets, and lamps make good targets. If these are taken apart, you can use a small battery-operated UV light to see evidence of the tampering.

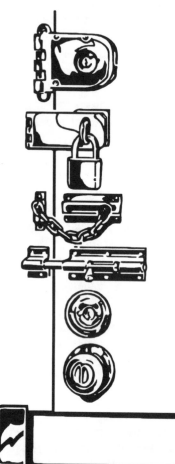

A dab of paint or fingernail polish will also let you keep a record of the position of such screws to see if they have been moved.

Books and upholstery buttons can have small dots of the same chemicals painted on them and checked now and then to see if they have been replaced. Battery-operated UV lights are available from The Spy Factory, Sherwood, and Edmund Scientific.

Small cracks in walls and openings between walls and windows or door frames, and the little plastic handles

"OLD SPARKY"
SPARK GAP TRANSMITTER

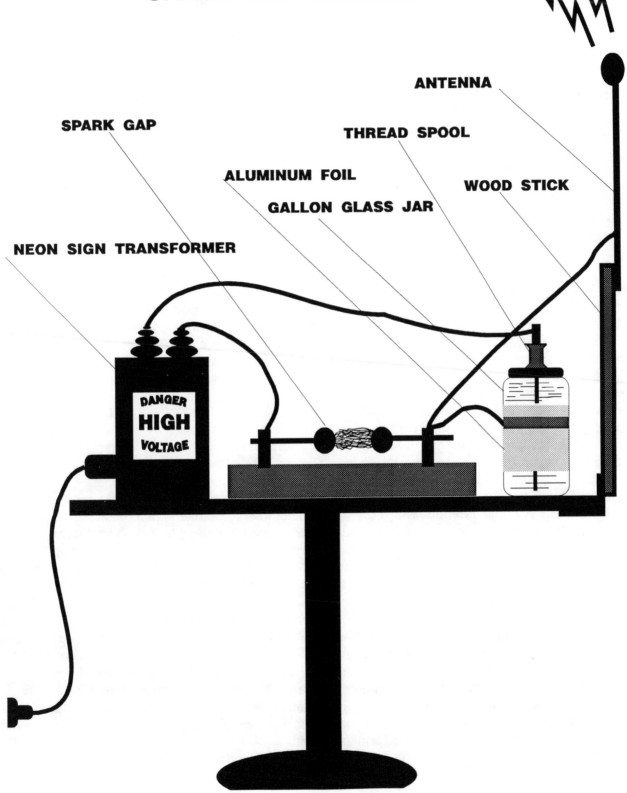

ANTENNA

SPARK GAP

THREAD SPOOL

ALUMINUM FOIL

WOOD STICK

GALLON GLASS JAR

NEON SIGN TRANSFORMER

DANGER
HIGH
VOLTAGE

on venetian blind cords, all of which could conceal a microphone or small bug, can be filled with caulk, putty, or silicone sealer. This keeps out more than one kind of bug.

OLD SPARKY

Old sparky is the name sometimes given to spark-gap transmitters (SGT) used back in the early years of this century for communicating with ships at sea. It produces a loud buzzing sound that jams a receiver being used to listen to a bug.

Unfortunately, it also interferes with everything else, such as "Monday Night Football," which could make you very unpopular in your neighborhood. Used in a rural area where there aren't any close neighbors, it is an effective method of preventing RF bugs from working.

You can make your own SGT, but keep in mind that it uses 10,000 volts or more. This is at very low current, but it is still dangerous. You need the following materials:

- One or more neon sign transformers
- A one-gallon glass jar for each transformer, with plastic lid
- A pound of salt for each jar
- Miscellaneous junk-a-line cord for the transformers, some metal rods (such as old curtain rods), empty thread spools, and several feet of wire. Look at the diagram and improvise, using what is available.

Fill the jar(s) with water and stir in as much salt as will dissolve. Dry the jar carefully, wrap several layers of aluminum foil around it, and tape it in place.

Find a metal rod for each jar (some old threaded rod found in the garage will work fine) and insert it through a hole in the lid. Use an empty thread spool or whatever to hold it in place—the rod should not touch the bottom of the jar.

The spark gap can be made from two pieces of brass rod (1/4 inch in diameter) or two large bolts held in place on a small piece of wood, such as a 2 x 4. Make it so one of the rods can be moved back and forth to adjust the width. Start with a gap of 1 inch for every 20,000 volts used.

Wire it as shown in the diagram. The connection to the foil on the jar can be two turns with the

insulation stripped off, or a metal band. The antenna can be a brass rod or whatever is handy.

When it is assembled, plug it in and watch the gap for a silver-blue spark. If there is no spark, unplug it and close the gap slightly until you get a spark.

One neon transformer is sufficient to jam bugs within a hundred yards. If you get carried away and use a dozen transformers, high-voltage plasma will be floating around all over the area, and someone could get zapped. The kid next door, for example, touches your screen door and gets bit. He goes home and tells his dad, who comes over and punches you out. A week later his wife has formed the first chapter of M.A.S.T. (Mothers Against Sparkgap Transmitters), and some congressperson sponsors a bill outlawing them without a federal license.

THE RF ROOM GUARD

The Room Guard is a device similar to a bug detector. It has a sensitivity control that is adjusted for the ambient (normal background) RF level in the room in which it is placed, and it triggers an alarm if this level is exceeded by someone bringing an RF device into the room. The Room Guard is available from Capri Electronics.

PHONE GUARDS

There are many devices available to help secure your phone lines.

- A privacy module locks out extension phones. The first phone that is picked up is the only one that works, keeping anyone from listening on an extension. This is also available from Capri.
- A listen-down amplifier alerts you to a hook bypass switch. This is the technique used by an infinity transmitter; it closes the phone cradle switch and turns on the microphone.

Any small audio amplifier works. The Electronic Rainbow has one in kit form for about $10.95. Hobby stores and new and surplus electronic dealers often have them already built for a few bucks more. Most of these little amps have the speaker attached, and all that has to be done to make it work is to connect two small capacitors to the input of the amp and to the phone line.

The device does not interfere with the phone, and if there is audio on the line when the phone is not being used, you can hear it and know that a hook switch bypass is in use.

• The digital voltmeter used in the REMOBS section is another inexpensive device for protecting your line. Place it on your desk where you can see it, and if anything should be attached to your line, it changes the reading and you'll notice it.

Such a meter can also be made to set off an alarm if the line voltage changes by a certain amount.

• A separate ringer, available from stores that sell telephones, can be placed on the line and a switch wired to the phone to turn it off or on. This electrically isolates it from the line and defeats a hook by-pass switch. At first, you will forget about the switch, and when you answer, will wonder why no one is on the other end, but soon you'll get used to it.

• There are devices that prevent the line voltage from dropping to the off-hook level that stop a drop-out relay from automatically turning a tape recorder on or activating line taps when the phone is lifted.

• Last but not least, the Telcom Security Unit does most of the above and defeats or detects various types of line taps. It is available from Sherwood.

TROJAN HORSES

Beware of spies bearing gifts. If some anonymous or suspicious person presents you with something that could contain a listening device, check it out, and remember that almost anything can hide a bug. The most likely one would be a table lamp or something that plugs into a wall socket.

Be suspicious of packages with cards asking you not to open them until Christmas—especially if you receive them in July.

LOOK AROUND

Using the above devices or techniques will make your home secure from inside devices. Now consider outside listening methods.

You already know how to detect and defeat lasers, and keeping the windows closed and drapes drawn will defeat directional microphones, but in the summer people like to open their windows. An open window won't reflect a laser beam, but other things inside the room can, such as a mirror.

To use a directional microphone the listener also will probably have an open window. Probably the smallest one available will be used, but it has to be as big as the reflector. If he can hear you, then you can hear him. The Gatling gun device discussed earlier can be built for under $200.

One way to use a parabolic is to leave it in plain sight. A neighbor installs a 4-foot dish on his roof, which you probably won't notice in the first place, but if you do, you'll absently think that your neighbor has installed a satellite TV dish on his roof and forget about it. Oh, maybe once in a while you might notice it, but you still won't give it any real thought, other than being jealous if you don't have satellite TV.

So one day, a week later, when you have stopped noticing it, it happens to come loose, and instead of pointing at Telstar, it now points at your living room window. But you don't notice . . .

A noise generator placed on the window sill makes it difficult for a listener to hear anything. Edmund Scientific has a sound generator that produces the sounds of rain, a waterfall, and surf, which is random sound and hard to tune out with an equalizer. It is pleasant to listen to (except by the spy across the street) and not distracting like radio or (ugh) TV.

Look for surveillance vans. Is there always a van parked near you? Or a panel truck or pickup with a camper? An amateur probably won't have more than one, but the feds have many and will probably switch them frequently. Perhaps you can find out who it is.

Do a little spying yourself. Write down license numbers and see if the same ones (but not necessarily on the same vehicles) are there at different times. If you see a van pull up and stop, watch it for a while. If the driver doesn't get out and go somewhere, then someone is probably watching someone. Use binoculars to watch them, but don't let them see you. See if they seem to be there in shifts.

Two pieces of advice: if it is a government surveillance, don't assume that you are the target; by now, you should have a good idea whether you are of any interest to any agency. Second, don't interfere. Interfering can get you into something you can't handle. There might be a drug bust coming down, and you could mess it up. This could end up in a drug dealer not being arrested, or it could result in someone getting hurt—maybe you. Stay out of it.

One way that you might find out who it is is to use a scanner. If you have the frequencies of the police and federal agencies, set it on the repeater input frequencies. You can only hear their radios if they are close. On UHF bands, the mobile units are almost always 5 mc. above the repeater output. If you live in a large city, try this on the local police band, which is probably from 460.050 to 460.550. Set it to search from 465.050 to 564.550. You can hear the signals direct from the police vehicles, not through the repeater, so they come in strong only if they are fairly close.

The frequencies used by both federal and local law enforcement in California, including many of the repeater input frequencies, are given in the book *Government Radio Systems* by Bob Kelty, available at Quement Electronics, or write Kelty at Mobile Radio Resources, 2661 Carol Drive, San Jose, CA 95125 for prices. It's available in book form and on computer disk. Other books have listings for other states.

WARNING: the Electronic Communications Privacy Act places some restrictions on listening. It seems to say that it is unlawful to listen to scrambled conversations, such as the DES used by the FBI and other federal agencies—even though you can't tell what they are saying. Possibly the reason is that they don't want anyone to tape-record them and keep them for decoding. But this is not going to happen with a 72-bit key.

Read it and see if you can decipher it (I can't) before you do this. Or see if you can find a lawyer who is familiar with this federal law.

If you can eliminate law enforcement as the spies, then there may well be something unlawful going on, and maybe you can do something about it. Just be sure you know what you are getting into.

These methods will make your home and office secure from spies. Now let's have a look at surveillance from the other perspective.

PART IX

OBTAINING SURVEILLANCE EQUIPMENT

Before you do any kind of surveillance, keep in mind three things. First, bugging a person for malicious or selfish reasons or to get even is morally wrong. Second, it is against the law. Third, it can get you threatened, beaten up, or shot—which, if you don't already know, isn't the most pleasant way to spend your time. Getting shot at tends not only to ruin one's day, but to make one consider backing off from such situations.

A number of devices that can be used for surveillance are available to anyone who has the money, and many can be homemade. Here are some devices people have used to bug others.

- *Wireless microphones and bugs.* Most of the wireless microphones and bugs that are available from stores and by mail order transmit on the FM broadcast band. The reason is that it is legal to use them as long as you're not listening to someone who does not know about it. The Federal Communications Commission (FCC) permits "low-power" devices to work in these areas, and, of course, almost everyone has an FM radio to use for listening to them.

Wireless microphones and other products can be used (legally) on many other frequencies, but they are less common because not everyone has a scanner that will receive them. But spies do. Some of the frequencies for these are listed in Appendix D.

- *Hearing aids.* Aids for the hearing impaired can be used as bugs. In a classroom or lecture hall, the transmitter is placed on the instructor's desk, and the receiver is used like a hearing aid. The range is often limited to a few hundred feet.

- *Baby monitors.* Some wireless baby monitors use an RF transmitter instead of the subcarrier method. Using a portable scanner, I have received them clearly three blocks from the source. I thought I was doing the users a favor when I called to tell them that their baby monitor was broadcasting their conversations around the neighborhood. They were anything but thankful, but they did stop using it.

- *Citizens band radios.* CB radios have been used as bugs. It is not difficult to take them apart and remove the receiver and case, and they can be small enough to hide in a number of places. Install a different crystal, and it transmits on a frequency that CB receivers and many scanners won't pick up. The same can be done with cordless phones.

- *Two-way radios.* Tyco makes a small two-way radio as part of its Spy-Tech toy line that can be used as a bug.

- *Transmitters used at fast-food drive-up windows.* This can also be used as a secret listening device.

A spy can modify and use any of these, or he can build bugs himself. Some libraries still have books with schematic diagrams of various types of bugs that can be built and used with a little knowledge and experience. Look in the card catalogue under "eavesdropping." The university libraries are a better place to look because such books are usually stolen from public libraries.

Schematic diagrams and other information needed to build a low-frequency transmitter can also be found in back issues of *Popular Electronics, Radio Electronics,* and other magazines.

Building them from just a diagram requires the ability to lay out the components and make and drill the circuit board, or perf board, but a number of kits are available that make them easier to build. Usually kits have a circuit board that is predrilled and a pictorial diagram that shows where to place the various parts. The only skills required are the ability to identify the components and to use a soldering iron, and no expensive test equipment is needed.

WHERE TO BUY SURVEILLANCE EQUIPMENT

Rainbow Kits has a wireless microphone kit that works both on and outside the FM band for $12.95 and a line-powered phone transmitter for $10.95.

Another bug, a little more advanced, can be made from the Motorola MC-2831A and MC-2833 chips. They are FM transmitters made for cordless phones. Add a few components and you have a complete bug. The chips sell for less than a dollar and the other parts for about $10.

A different crystal can be used to make it transmit on a frequency in the TV channel 2 band, near the sound portion of the signal. The characteristics of the TV signal make it much more difficult to find, and it can be missed by some bug detectors, unless they are being used by experienced operators. This is the snuggling method mentioned earlier.

Crystals are available from Jameco Electronics and some surplus stores. Check *Nuts and Volts* magazine listings.

These chips can also work in the low- and medium-frequency bands. MF has an area from 1.61 to 1.705 mc. where low-power devices are legal to operate, or with a different crystal it can transmit below the AM broadcast band, where some bug detectors will not find them.

The 2833 chip has an extra unused transistor, and by adding a few more components, it is possible to increase the power output to about 250 milliwatts which, with a decent antenna, should transmit for at least several blocks.

The microphone can be from a hearing aid. Some dealers have older or broken hearing aids that they will sell for a few dollars or give away. The hearing aids also contain other useful parts.

Read a few books on basic electronics, schematic diagrams, and identifying components (resistors, transistors, etc.). Practice with the Rainbow kits, and you may be able to build a bug from the Motorola chips.

For less than $30, you have a sophisticated bug that would cost hundreds of dollars from a "dealer" (if you could find one). If you want to have a technician make something for you, consider calling a community college or other school and hiring a second year work-study electronics student.

To listen to such bugs, it is not necessary to spend $425 on a new scanner. Pawn shops frequently have used scanners and shortwave receivers for less than $100.

Nuts and Volts magazine also has ads for used receivers and a list of electronic flea markets that have used equipment.

If you want something better, go to a dealer that specializes in communications equipment. He should have a wide variety to choose from and professional salespeople who know their business to help you find the right model.

In California, try Quement Electronics in San José or Scanners Unlimited in San Carlos; EEB in the Washington, D.C., area is one of the largest, and Scanner World has a large selection and a free catalogue. Others are listed in Appendix C.

USING SURVEILLANCE DEVICES

If someone decided to bug you, how would he go about doing it? Obtaining a bug is one thing; using it is another. Once he has one, where is he going to hide it? How easily can he access your office or home? How much time will he have? Does he have a way to get in to have a look first? What does he know about you?

Knowing where the most useful information is going to come from makes a difference in where the microphone should be placed. The acoustics of the room should be considered, if possible, as this can affect the quality of the sound it transmits.

Placing a bug behind a picture in a room with otherwise bare walls makes for sound that can be more difficult to understand because of the echoes it picks up, but it can be installed quickly.

The best results are from a microphone that is very close to where the speaker will be. On a desk is an excellent location, such as in a penholder or desk organizer, but if long range is needed or the bug needs to function for a long period of time, then either more space (for batteries) or access to the power line is needed.

If it is to be placed inside a lamp, the one closest to a couch, easy chair, or desk will probably get the best audio, but if the lamp is to contain the modulator described above, it has to be somewhere that light can be seen from outside.

An experienced spy will consider all these things.

The section on physical searching provided much information on where someone might hide a bug. Here are a few more examples.

For short-term surveillance, a disposable bug can be tossed into a wastebasket. You are an attorney and an important client has an appointment with you. The opposition finds out, and it has someone drop in and ask to see you for "only a minute on a very important matter" just before that appointment. The visitor makes up a story or discovers that he made a mistake and has the wrong attorney. He leaves, and you are puzzled or irritated—and also bugged. Meanwhile, another client is in the waiting room listening to you.

Inside a hollowed-out book is another good place, as mentioned earlier. Such books are available at places like the Spy Factory. A small hole is punched in the spine to let the sound in, and the microphone is glued against the hole.

Consider which book to use. Old novels, once read, are more likely to be left on the shelf than reference books. A lawyer who bugs a lawyer or an architect who bugs an architect will have a good idea of which books are likely to be found but seldom used. Switching books and dust jackets take but a few seconds.

Some mattresses have little air vents covered with wire mesh—perfect for letting sound in. A small incision can be made in the fabric and the bug slipped inside and secured with glue, Velcro, or some other adhesive, making sure the microphone is facing the vent. A small piece of the material can be removed from a corner of the mattress or from under the "do not remove" tag that most people do not remove and glued over the opening. It is unlikely to be noticed.

Small two-sided makeup mirrors with metal frames can hide bugs. There is enough space between the mirrors, the small hole where the frame is joined lets sound in, and the wire base makes a decent antenna.

Many stereo speakers have thick foam front panels that are held in place with Velcro. A small piece of the foam can be cut out with a sharp knife and the bug hidden there, which is one of the best places for a bug—except, of course, when the stereo is on. The foam lets all the sound through, is at the right level to hear voices, and can be installed in a minute.

Some speakers sit on small stands, and a bug can be hidden on the bottom of the enclosure with Scotch-mount adhesive. It probably won't be noticed until spring cleaning.

I once heard about a bug that was built into a false bottom of a wastebasket. Only 1/2-inch deep, which no one would notice, the false bottom contained a homemade transmitter with a series of calculator batteries and had four holes in the edge to let the sound in.

Periodically when the batteries got low, the janitor in a large office building was told to switch it with another one and take the bugged one to an office on a different floor and leave it. Later, he was told to switch them again. This went on for years, so the story goes. It's probably true. When is the last time you paid any attention to a wastebasket?

Probably the most clever method of hiding a bug that I know of was one that was built into a large black candle. Part of the inside was carefully melted out from the bottom and the bug (a modified FM wireless microphone with a one-stage transistor amplifier) and two D-cell batteries were placed inside. The antenna was a piece of coat hanger, cut to the precise wavelength for better transmission, heated over a gas stove, and inserted partway into the candle. Then the wax was replaced. A ribbon was placed around it (to hide the microphone and let the sound in) and then warmed at the edges so it stuck to the wax and wouldn't fall off.

The most unusual place for a bug to be hidden that I ever heard is from a story told by a former federal agent, who swears it really happened. For a long time, certain people had been trying to bug someone without success. He was too careful to say anything incriminating anywhere someone could be listening. So what these people did was have one of their female personnel get close to him, and after a while, he began to trust her a little. Then, when they thought he was about to reveal something they wanted to know, she arranged to meet him on a topless beach in California.

Now, there isn't any way to hide a bug on a girl wearing a topless string bikini, right? Wrong. The antenna was hidden inside the strings, and the rest of the bug was . . . internal. Imagination is the only limit to where a bug can be hidden.

THE LISTENING POST

Someone has managed to install a bug in your office. Now where is he going to set up a listening post? This has a lot to do with the type of device selected.

If the listener has an office or apartment next to or directly above or below you, a small wireless microphone will probably work fine. If his listening post is across the street, a high-quality wireless microphone or infrared device is more effective for the job.

A temporary post can be in the phone distribution closet or the maintenance area if the spy has regular access to the area, can use a tape recorder, and can replace the tapes as they become full.

A converted cordless phone will transmit at least a block with a good antenna (such as a curtain rod), so if the listener is that close, he can use one of these.

A van equipped with the necessities (refrigerator, chemical toilet, and communication equipment) is the perfect listening post, as it can be within easy listening range of the target—assuming the spy can find a parking place.

If there is a park near the target, an eavesdropper may buy some thrift-store clothes and become homeless for a while. A pocket-size tape recorder will capture the conversation.

If the feds have set up a post, it will probably be large; an office or apartment rented on a temporary basis. There will likely be six agents assigned to it—three teams of two—and three tape recorders, the large open-reel type, which requires a fair amount of space.

If a repeater system is used, the listening post will be a long distance away. They are too expensive for short transmission. A series phone tap has a low output, so the listening post will be in a neighbor's house or adjacent apartment but not much further.

Use what you can come up with in the profile of the probable spies, estimate the probable distance the bug can transmit (based on information from earlier chapters), and look inside this area. Are there business rivals or other known enemies within the range?

PART X
USING INTERCEPTED
INFORMATION

The whole purpose of surveillance is to obtain useful information. Sometimes a listening device produces information that doesn't seem worth anything at the time, but it might become very useful.

An experienced spy tape-records everything he hears and keeps every scrap of information he obtains from any source. He will label, date, and store it for cross-referencing. It is all part of the picture the spy is trying to create. This is one of the "secrets" of intelligence. (The other is that there are no secrets.)

An experienced spy is also careful about how he uses what he hears. If someone suspects he is being listened to, he can draw him out. If one contractor consistently underbids another by a very small amount, someone is going to get suspicious—and maybe get even.

In a lawsuit, if one party always seems to be one step ahead of the other, the latter may suspect surveillance and take appropriate action.

He admitted at the deposition that he had been digging through their trash for several months. He produced a box of scraps of paper he had found. The scraps didn't contain all the information he had amassed, but they didn't check it that thoroughly and didn't know that. If they had, they would have known that he had to have another source of information. He had joined the religious organization pretending to have an interest in their perverse philosophy. His real interest was researching the organization for a book and to find out what had happened to a friend who had joined them. He bugged their offices, and this was the source they never realized he had.

Some victims of surveillance simply destroy any devices they find. Some call in the feds. Others have their own way of dealing with spies. In the above example, someone (an amateur) wasn't as careful as he might have been. There were times when he "knew too much," and it almost cost him his life. To stop his research, someone shot at him and threatened him in other ways.

SURVEILLANCE AND PRIVACY
IN THE FUTURE

The latest development in making electronic devices smaller is called direct mount. An integrated circuit, or chip, is actually only about 1/32-inch square, which is too small to connect wires to. To make it easier to use, it is placed inside a plastic or ceramic package with two rows of pins that easily fit onto a printed circuit board. This is called the dual inline package, or DIP. The new direct-mount technology places the chip directly on the printed circuit board, which eliminates the need for the bulky package.

Through the use of direct-mount technology, the burst transmitter can be made as small as a postage stamp and can store sound for an hour or more.

Another new development is the molded-plastic circuit board that can be made in any shape, such as a wall outlet, to hide the burst transmitter. It sends its signal through the air like any RF bug or through the power lines and is almost impossible to find. Mass-produced by companies like Intel and Motorola, these boards are very affordable.

Microminiature bugs the size of an aspirin tablet

are powered by a beam of microwave energy and so require no battery. They transmit a hundred feet or so and can be used alone or with a repeater.

Microwave beams penetrate walls and closed windows and are reflected off the air inside a target room to reveal everything spoken there to the listener a mile away. Only a very expensive receiver or spectrum analyzer will detect them.

Computer-enhanced techniques used to reconstruct and enhance video images from space probes have been adapted to improve the sound received from improved lasers and other audio listening devices.

Supersensitive receivers with high-gain directional antennas pick up the radiation from TEMPEST secure computers allowing the user to intercept and store anything on the screen.

Supersophisticated debugging equipment will be invented to find the new surveillance devices, which will again be improved, and better debugging gear will follow, and the game goes on . . .

• • •

In 1952, President Harry Truman created, by way of a supersecret memorandum, the National Security Agency, which for many years the government denied even existed. The present administration could as easily create another supersecret agency for the purpose of domestic spying. This could be done because drug-related crime is a "clear and present danger to the structure and existence of the government," and the agency would not be subject to the Omnibus Act or other laws against electronic surveillance. Neither the people nor the Congress would know about it.

MAYBE THEY ALREADY HAVE . . .
Quis custodiet ipsos custodes?

THE STORY OF A BUGGING

About ten years ago, an employee of a medium-size manufacturing company in the Pacific Northwest began working on a plan to burglarize his employer. He planned to steal information about the company's manufacturing methods and other proprietary and technical data. He admitted this when he was confronted by company officials. All of the details of this plot are not available, but some of them are as follows.

The factory was in a secluded location, dark and deserted at night. Security guards made rounds of the area, and the police drove through periodically, but there were long periods of time when no one was there. This made it an easier target.

Photograph one shows the general location of the plant. The factory is at the left center, seen over the guard rail. The company did not want a closer picture that would identify it to be published. This is typical and illustrates a point: most people who have been bugged don't want anyone to know about it. Would you? Because of this, the vast majority of buggings are never publicized and the public has no idea how common it is.

Photograph 2 shows the front of the apartment building in which a company supervisor lived at the time of the bugging.

Photograph 3 shows the window on the left where the microphone was hidden. The bushes completely cover the corner of the building.

Photograph 4 was taken inside the apartment. The wood frame window was broken. The owner of the building kept promising to fix it, but like many landlords, he was too stingy to spend the money if he could avoid it. It was spring, the weather was warm, and so the supervisor did not complain often enough to force the owner to take care of it.

At the top of photograph 5 are wires that were once used to power a light fixture, which was broken and had been taken down. The wires were still hot and were used to power the bug.

Thin speaker wire led around the corner of the building, hidden in the crack between the top of the back door frame and the stucco wall and then down to the ground. From there it was buried under the loose dirt and leaves to where the bug was hidden behind the rhododendron bush. The bug was a homemade transmitter that operated on 330 mc. with an estimated range of half a mile.

This transmitter could have been powered by a large battery, which could have been hidden easily. Why the bugger used the wiring from the old light fixture is not known, but he could have reached the wires by standing on the railing around the small back porch just a few feet to the left of the broken window without anyone being able to see him because of all the bushes.

How he knew about the broken window and why he believed it would not be fixed soon are also unknown. Possibly, he first intended to use a contact microphone on one of the panes but changed his mind when he discovered the one that wouldn't close. The device wasn't noticed until a storm blew the shrubs away from the wall.

Photograph 6 is another view of the bushes. On the right is a white house. This is where the bugger

Photograph No. 1

Photograph No. 2

Photograph No. 3

Photograph No. 4

Photograph No. 5

Photograph No. 6

had his listening post. He was a temporary resident of the property. Because he lived too far away from the supervisor's apartment for a bug to transmit, he rented the garage from the people who lived there.

When the supervisor noticed the wire, he followed it and found the transmitter. The supervisor did not know of anyone who would want to bug him and didn't know how long the listening device had been in place since the window had been broken for so long.

He finally concluded that it had something to do with the company and probably was part of a plan to rob or burglarize it, so he reported the incident to the owners. They called a security expert who used a frequency meter to see where the bug was transmitting and advised them to try to draw the bugger out.

Among the mistakes the bugger made were letting people know that he was interested in short-wave radio listening and using the frequency he did. As stated in the section on using a scanner to find bugs, receivers that will tune this area have been widely available for only a few years, and this incident took place in the early eighties.

The countersurveillance plan had the supervisor leak information that the company was going to do something, which they believed would cause the suspected thief to act. The plan worked, and the company employee was caught in the act. He was "dealt with" by the supervisor and some other company employees.

Bugging people can be hazardous to one's health.

APPENDIX B

EQUIPMENT

FROM CAPRI ELECTRONICS

ADVANCED TRANSMITTER (BUG) DETECTOR

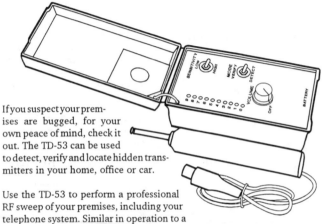

If you suspect your premises are bugged, for your own peace of mind, check it out. The TD-53 can be used to detect, verify and locate hidden transmitters in your home, office or car.

Use the TD-53 to perform a professional RF sweep of your premises, including your telephone system. Similar in operation to a Geiger counter, the sensitive antenna system can be used to probe all areas of a room. As the antenna approaches the hidden transmitter, the audible tone clicks faster and faster while the ten step solid-state meter indicates the signal strength.

At this point, switch modes from *Detect* to *Verify* to differentiate a bug from a regular radio or TV transmission. If a bugging device is present, a continuous squealing tone is generated by the TD-53. By sweeping the probe, this tone can lead you directly to the bug. The switch selectable *SENSITIVITY* level improves detection capabilities of the unit in high signal strength areas. For private (non-alerting) listening, an earphone jack is provided.

Included with the TD-53 is the P-01 wideband active probe which covers 5 MHz to 1,000 MHz. The P-01 can be positioned up to 25 feet away from the TD-53 by using an extension cable. For example, the probe could be discreetly placed in a target room while the TD-53 is monitored in another room.

Several other plug-in probes are available which will extend the usefulness of your TD-53. (See page 5 of this catalog.)

The unit measures 5.8" x 3.4 x 2" (with cover closed) and weights 9 oz. It is powered by one 9 volt alkaline battery (included). Also included is an illustrated instruction manual.

PHONE STROBE FLASHER

This solid state strobe flashes brightly whenever the phone rings. It is ideal for use in noisy locations to let you know the phone is ringing.

Modular connections for easy installation. Phone line powered – no batteries required. Can be used on single and two line systems, but only line 1 (the red/green pair) will flash.

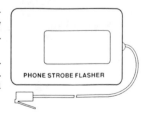

PHONE STROBE FLASHER

FROM CAPRI ELECTRONICS

ANSWERING MACHINE STOPPER

Eliminate the annoyance of picking up your phone while the message on the answering machine is playing. This device stops the recorded message as soon as any phone in the house is picked up and allows the answering machine to reset itself.

Easy modular connection. Works on single and two line systems. On two line systems, the answering machine must be connected to line 1 (the red/green pair). Only one unit is required and it is plugged in at the answering machine location.

MICROWAVE DETECTOR

As new threats to your privacy are put into use, we develop new products to counter them. The TD-24 is designed to detect the new RF transmitters (bugs) that operate in the low microwave bands.

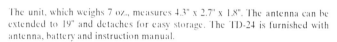

In use, the TD-24 warns you of the presence of nearby microwave transmitters in the frequency range of 800 MHz to 2500 MHz (2.5 GHz) by the *RF ALERT* LED. The flashing *RANGE* LED and audio tone give an indication of the distance to the bug. (The closer you get to the bug, the faster the LED flashes and the tone clicks.) The *SENSITIVITY* control, along with the two LEDs, helps you quickly zero in on hidden microwave bugs.

A special filter circuit keeps the TD-24 from being activated falsely by signals outside the microwave band. Due to the characteristics of microwaves, three sweeps of the room should be made with the TD-24 antenna adjusted to different lengths as covered in the instructions.

The unit, which weighs 7 oz., measures 4.3" x 2.7" x 1.8". The antenna can be extended to 19" and detaches for easy storage. The TD-24 is furnished with antenna, battery and instruction manual.

TELEPHONE PRIVACY MODULE

With a TPM-1 on each phone in the house, the first person to pick up the phone is the only one who can use the line until that phone is hung up. No one can listen in on other extensions; thus preventing eavesdropping.

Also useful for preventing interruptions to modem transmissions that can be caused by picking up an extension while the modem is in use. Installs easily with a modular plug on one end and a modular jack on the other end. For single line phones only. Order one for each phone in your house.

FROM CAPRI ELECTRONICS
VIDEO CAMERA DETECTOR

Because video surveillance is becoming more common, you need to be able to detect that type of privacy invasion. The VCD-41 can help you quickly determine if hidden surveillance cameras are being used in any room.

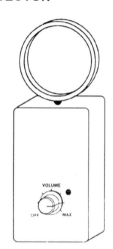

Video cameras radiate a signal which can be picked up by the VCD-41's directional loop antenna and converted to an audible tone. This tone is heard in the earphones (included). The tone increases in volume as you get closer to the camera. By turning the unit with its directional antenna, you can pinpoint the camera's location. Our tests with various cameras have shown a detection range in excess of 12 feet.

The VCD-41 measures 7.5" (with antenna attached) x 2.7" x 1.8", weighs 7 oz. and is furnished complete with 9 volt alkaline battery, earphones and instructions.

RF ROOM GUARD™

Once you set the RF Room Guard for the ambient RF level in a room, it will go to an alarm condition if the RF level in the room (in the range of 1 MHz to 2.5 GHz) increases. This will alert you to the possibility of an RF bug having been carried in by a visitor or planted while you were away. Ideal for use in conference rooms or other areas that need to be secured.

The RF Room Guard can also warn you if your telephone has been bugged with an RF transmitter. If the unit consistantly alarms when you use your telephone, chances are good that an RF bug has been wired in to the phone.

The alarm condition is indicated by a red LED on the front panel. The unit also has an alarm interface that provides both powered (12 VDC) and dry contacts for connecting remote indicators.

The *RF LEVEL* meter gives you a relative reading of the RF signal level in your area. This can also help you determine if an RF bug has been installed nearby.

Controls include *SENSITIVITY* for adjusting for the room's background RF level and *ALARM SET* for adjusting the level at which the alarm will turn on.

An optional Alarm Module gives both an adjustable audible alarm and a flashing visual alarm. It comes with 15 feet of cable. A longer cable can be used if desired. Since it measures only 2.2" x 3.5" x 1.5", it can be placed most anywhere that a remote indicator is desired. The Alarm Module is easily wired to the alarm interface on back of the RF Room Guard.

FROM SHERWOOD COMMUNICATIONS

COMMUNICATIONS INTEGRITY DEVICE

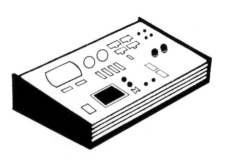

At last a comprehensive instrument and line analyzer for complete telephone security. The Communications Integrity Device (CID-90) was conceived and developed to meet the growing challenges to maintain communications integrity. Designed by TSCM professionals to combat the intrusive threats brought about by rapid developments in communications technology, advanced attacks and other vulnerabilities. The CID-90 uses proprietary LSI circuitry (equivalent to many thousands of transistors) to provide the utmost reliability and flexibility. It is built in a rugged aluminum case, 7″ x 12⅞″ x 2¾″. A sturdy discrete standard locking attache case provides ample room for the unit and all accessories and options. Lightweight unit (only 17 pounds) including accessories.

The CID-90 features the following advances. Any two wires may be accessed for direct testing. An auto ranging panel meter is used to record test results. A 120 Ohm phantom standard load may be placed across any wire pair by a separate control. An Ultra High Gain Audio Amp circuit with filter, facilitates all testing. A separate line driver provides excitation voltage for carbon mics. In addition, the CID-90 contains a polarity reversal control, RF section with a range of 10-750 KHz and a sensitivity of 6 uV. System incorporates line tracers with two types of tones, including silent (ultrasonic), non-alerting supplied with receiver and audio oscillator for conventional testing. Includes comprehensive manual covering standard, electronic and key telephones.

Battery powered for portability by commonly available batteries. A built in battery condition meter assures uninterupted testing. Connections are facilitated by jacks, cords and test clips. Tape recorder output provides for evidence recordings. To enhance the CID-90's capabilities, wire access is provided by an insulated BNC connector, five way binding posts allowing series or parallel access and test ports. These features enable the operator to connect additional equipment used in advanced techniques such as Oscilloscope, Datascope, Vectorscope, Countersurveillance Receivers, Spectrum Analyzers and Time Domain Reflectometers.

The CID-90 detects RF taps, Direct attacks, tape recorder switches, data leakage, instrument manipulation, frame room attacks, system manipulation, system vulnerabilities, audio leakage, duals, constant line monitors, burglar alarms, phantom transmitters, passive by-passes and dialed number recorders.

CID-90 will also perform the following tests: On-Hook/Off Hook-voltage and current, all wire listen, phantom transmitter detection, loop current, balance testing, resistance and capacitance.

LUNAR LIGHT CAMERAS

Lunar light low night level camera features single stage Image Intensifier and 1″ Newvicon (body only, without lens). Extremely high sensitivity operation; useable picture 3 x 10-4 footcandles. Resolution of more than 600 lines at center; low blooming and low image retention; built in RS-170 LSI sync generator, automatic beam control, automatic electronic focus control, automatic gain control. Heavy-duty die-cast construction.

PINHOLE LENSES

Designed for use on concealed cameras, the Pinhole Lenses are useful in any Undercover surveillance work. Compact size and minimal front exposure ensure discreet observation.

No. 5020	Straight Pinhole Lens:	9.0mm/F3.4
No. 5021	R.A. Pinhole Lens:	9.0mm/F3.4
No. 6000	Straight Pinhole Lens:	5.5mm/F3.0
No. 6001	R.A. Pinhole Lens:	5.5mm/F3.0
No. 6002	Straight Pinhole Lens:	11mm/F2.3
No. 6003	R.A. Pinhole Lens:	11mm/F2.3
No. 6004	Camcorder/35mm Lens:	8mm/F2.0
No. 6005	Camcorder/35mm Lens:	11mm/F2.0

AUTO IRIS ALSO AVAILABLE

SPRINKLER HEAD SURVEILLANCE

Pinhole lens disguised in a standard pendent fire sprinkler head. The lens has an adjustable iris and head to see in any 360 degree direction. Adjustable downward and to the side by moving a set screw. Two focal lengths available. The 11mm f/2.5 sees a field of view of 10' x 13.5' at 15 feet. The 22mm "sees" 5' x 6.5' at 15 feet. Easy to install. Attaches to all "C" mount cameras. COMPLETE with ceiling mount.

MINI-CHIP CAMERA

Miniature CCD chip camera for easy concealment and mounting in tight places. Solid-state design requires no maintenance; estimated camera life is 10 years. 12 VDC or 110 VAC power makes the CCD a natural choice for use in vehicles and applications requiring portability or battery backup. Features C mount lens and auto exposure system. Resolution: Vertical 350; Horizontal 400. Sensitivity: Minimum illumination 3 Lux at F/1.4. Power consumption: 0.3 Watts. 1.25″ x 1.25″ x 4.0″. Several Models Available.

FROM SHERWOOD COMMUNICATIONS

STEALTH BODY WIRE SYSTEM

As versatile as it is rugged and dependable, the Stealth Body Wire System should be your first choice when concealment, plus high performance and reliability are the criteria. The system assures crisp, clear wireless operation, up to one-quarter mile, for listening or recording. Applications include: buys, investigative reporting and protection of undercover officers.

System receiver features automatic remote or manual operation. Six channel capability allows the receiver to monitor six different frequencies with a flip of a switch. A five position audio filter allows the person monitoring to switch various filters in and out in order to reduce background noises. Audio control include volume, squelch, and tone. A signal strength meter allows for visual review of incoming signals. Dedicated monitoring can be conducted with an ⅛ earphone or headphone monitoring with the ¼ earphone. The sealed, lead acid battery provides long life power. May be recharged with 12VDC or 110 VAC power source. Accessories include receiving crystal, COR receiver/recording cable, 110 VAC charging cable, auto lighter cable, telescoping antenna and sturdy carrying case.

The transmitter operates in the frequency range of 150 to 174 MHz. The transmitter also includes an external microphone jack. Audio AGC with on/off switch helps to maintain constant deviation and noise level. Rechargeable NiCad battery provides 100 mW RF power output for approximately two hours when fully charged. Ruggedly constructed and completely self-contained in heavy guage aluminum.

STEALTH SYSTEM OPTIONS

Additional options enhance the overall system performance of the Stealth System.

ATTACHE CASE RECORDING SYSTEM

Superb recording briefcase permits the full use of the briefcase while simultaneously providing clandestine and surreptitious recording capabilities. Choose your tape recorder from our stock. Features supersensitive hidden microphone. The recorder is started and stopped externally.

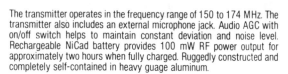

No. 4041 Attache Case Recorder (Leather)
No. 4042 Attache Case Recorder (Samsonite)

SPECIAL OPERATIONS RECORDER

Specially modified portable cassette recorder recorder for special operations. Easy to use voice actuation prevents silent gaps to save you tape and time. Features regular and half speed to double the recording time, 1 7/8 and 15/16th IPS. Cue/review finds selections with ease. Includes auto-level for perfect volume playback, tape counter, mike switch and mic jack for powering electret mics. Remote jack has zero current drain to preserve battery on telephone installations.

No. 5035 Special Operations Recorder
No. 2501 D-120 Tape
No. 9003 AC Power Supply
No. 9001 12 VDC Vehicle Adapter

UNDERCOVER VEHICLE VIDEO SYSTEM

Mounts specialized camera discreetly in trunk of car. Remote control system/monitor, located in the driver's compartment, controls the video cameras rotation, elevation, zoom and focus. All activities are viewed on a 3″ screen. The camera's ovjective lens is concealed behind a simulated side marker. The camera's pan and tilt movements occur at the lens' front element, enabling the system to view through small openings yet allowing for a wide range of motion. Supplied with a 12VDC camera, auto iris zoom lens, 8 hour tape deck, output for RF, cables, and installation manual.

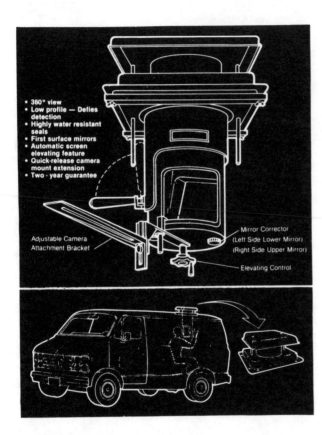

- 360° view
- Low profile — Defies detection
- Highly water resistant seals
- First surface mirrors
- Automatic screen elevating feature
- Quick-release camera mount extension
- Two - year guarantee

Adjustable Camera Attachment Bracket

Mirror Corrector
(Left Side Lower Mirror)
(Right Side Upper Mirror)

Elevating Control

The Van Periscope is designed to look like a standard air vent on a camper or van. It is a perfectly concealed viewing device. The system offers 360 degrees of rotation and 30 degrees of vertical correction, and is undetectable in close situations. The wire concealment screen is retractable, allowing for covert and undetactable viewing.

It is supplied with a universal camera mount which will accomodate still, video, telephoto and night vision applications. All camera and lens combinations of any size can be attached to the extension mount. The camera mount can be installed or removed in seconds.

Effective video can be recorded with the periscope extended only 1 inch above the roof of the surveillance vehicle. A standard 14″ x 14″ air vent conceals the Van Periscope and makes it undetectable in close surveillance situations.

Other outstanding features of the Van Periscope include the use of first surface mirrors on all optics, highly water resistant seals to protect the system integrity and an automatic screen elevating machanism.

Specifications:

Weight. . . . . 18 lbs.
Viewing Area. . . . . 360 degrees
Protrusion Above Roof . . . . 7″
Vertical Correction. . . . . 30 degrees
Installation: Fits into 14″ x 14″ air vent opening.

Camera Mount:

Horizontal adjustment . . . . 19″
Vertical adjustment. . . . . 7″
Quick releasing.

CARRIER CURRENT SOUND MONITOR

The smart electronic babysitter - listen from another room. Hear without actually being there! For use in homes, offices and industrial facilities. Just plug it into any AC outlet and monitor all activites. Receiver has volume control.

TIME-TEC

Time-Tec is a self-contained digital clock and an advanced high-tech R.F. detection circuit to detect any radio transmitting bugging devices within the range of 20 MHz to 1 GHz. Operates on AC current and is capable of detection within a 6 foot to 50 foot range. Clock time display blanks out in the presence of a bug leaving only the colon between the hour and minute. When the device is no longer present, the correct time will automatically return to the clock. Features fully functional alarm mode and battery back-up. Includes instructions and test transmitter.

R.F. TRANSMITTER & TAPE RECORDER DETECTOR

Designed to be worn on the body, the pocket size detector features a silent mode vibrator that is totally covert in operation. Instantly alerts you to the presence of a recorder or bug which is identified by the visual LED's located on the panel. Features dual mode wristwand antenna, silent vibrator alert. LED's, test transmitter, low battery indicator and self-contained rechargeable battery pack. Rugged, aircraft construction. Test transmitter included.

BUG DETECTOR/LOCATOR

Quietly and accurately detect and locate R.F. bugging devices in telephones, vehicles, boats, rooms, aircraft or concealed on the body. Because of the auto function, the BD/L has successfully detected eavesdropping signals in both strong R.F. signal areas as well as simpler environments by nontechnical personnel. Portable, battery powered unit operates in 1-1000 MHz range. Includes headphones, earphones, test transmitter, battery, vinyl case and instructions.

TELEMONITOR 2000

The Telemonitor 2000 utilizes advanced logic-chip technology, enabling you to discreetly listen in on your premises from any tone telephone in the world. Unlike other products, it does not require an activating beeper or whistle. Allows up to four units per line to be attached and is compatible with virtually all telephone exchanges in use in the U.S. Sensitive microphone will pick up whispers at 35 feet. Features an area select knob. Equipped with modular plugs. Requires no batteries. Will not affect normal incoming and outgoing calls even while monitoring.

TELEPHONE WATCHMAN

Remote activation feature allows the user to telephone from virtually anywhere in the world and listen to what is happening at another location. Activated by standard touchtones with unique 4-digit codes. Sensitive microphone detects the faintest of sounds ranging from hushed conversation to a water faucet left running - all with excellent clarity. Includes a detachable mi-Capable of remoting the mic over a crophone and detailed instructions. 100′ distance. 3″ x 4″ x1″.

ACOUSTIC NOISE GENERATOR

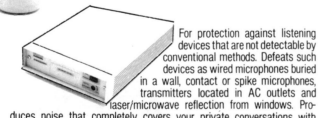

For protection against listening devices that are not detectable by conventional methods. Defeats such devices as wired microphones buried in a wall, contact or spike microphones, transmitters located in AC outlets and laser/microwave reflection from windows. Produces noise that completely covers your private conversations with unfilterable sound. Includes one transducer and various connectors for coupling walls, ceilings or air ducts. Capable of driving up to four transducers. 1.7″ x 6.0″ x 10.0″. 3 LB.

ULTRAVIOLET INSPECTION LIGHT

This compact long wave ultraviolet lamp is the smallest in the world. The lamp measures only 6¼ inches long by 2⅛ inches wide and is only ¾ inches thick. This 4 watt ultraviolet lamp operates on four (4) AA alkaline batteries, which are easily replaced. Rugged, thermoplastic lamp housing guarantees years of dependable service. Ideal for thief detection purposes, re-admission control and a must for TSCM inspections.

NVEC-500 POCKETSCOPE

The NVEC 500 second generation viewer is one of the smallest, lightest and highest performance hand held night vision instruments currently available. It utilizes a 18mm second generation, MCP wafer type image intensifier. This tube provides self-limiting brightness which eliminates blooming and streaking whenever bright objects are in the field of view.

The NVEC 500 is supplied with a 2 X 50mm objective lens and can be coupled to any C-mount lens. This allows various optical configurations using low cost standard 'C' mount lenses. The eyepiece is adjustable to compensate for any visual requirement.

This extremely compact unit is available with factory new, or reconditioned-selected grade intensifiers for significant optical cost savings. Shipped with carrying case, battery, and operating instructions.

SPECIFICATIONS

OPTICAL

Magnification	1X, 2X or 3X
Diopter Range	+3 to -4

IMAGE TUBE

Type	MX-9916
Resolution	28 Lp/mm
Photocathode	S-20R
Gain	7,000 Min.-15,000 Max.

MECHANICAL

Length	5.3 in.
Width	~2 in.
Height	3 in.
Weight	10 oz.

ELECTRICAL

Power	3 VDC.
Battery	2 "AA"
Battery Life	25 - 30 Hrs.

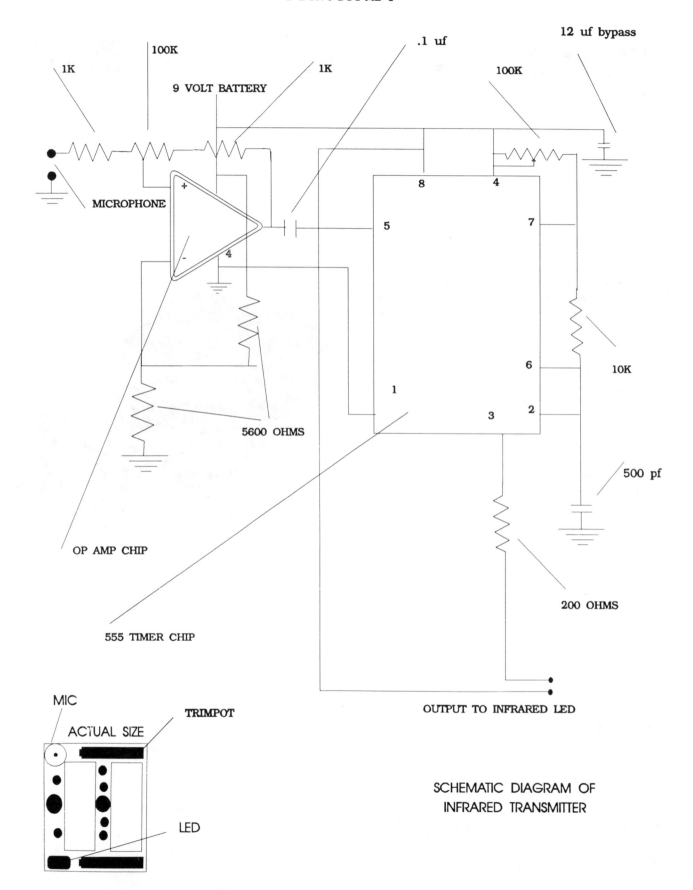

SCHEMATIC DIAGRAM OF
INFRARED TRANSMITTER

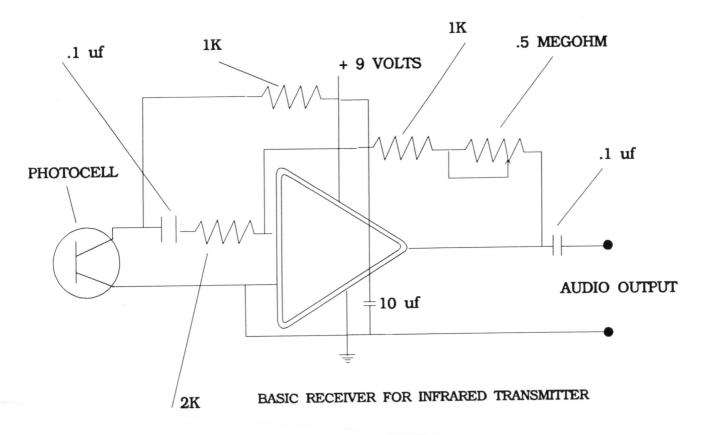

BASIC RECEIVER FOR INFRARED TRANSMITTER

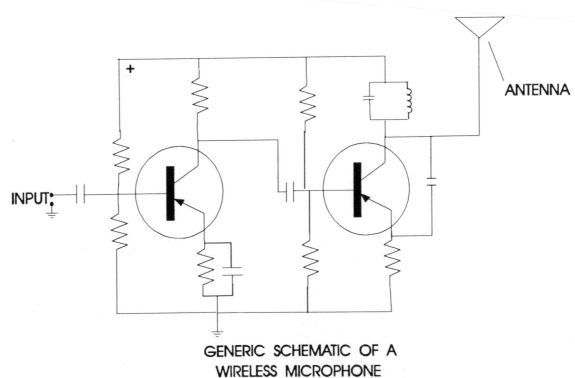

GENERIC SCHEMATIC OF A
WIRELESS MICROPHONE
IT HAS ONLY 14 PARTS

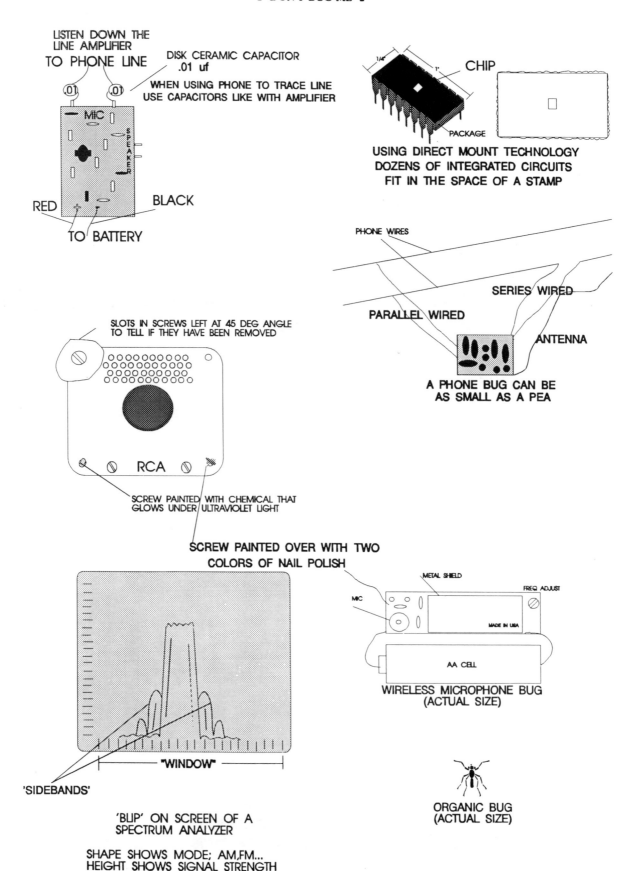

LISTEN DOWN THE
LINE AMPLIFIER
TO PHONE LINE

DISK CERAMIC CAPACITOR
.01 uf

WHEN USING PHONE TO TRACE LINE
USE CAPACITORS LIKE WITH AMPLIFIER

MIC
SPEAKER
RED
BLACK
TO BATTERY

CHIP
1/4" 1"
PACKAGE

USING DIRECT MOUNT TECHNOLOGY
DOZENS OF INTEGRATED CIRCUITS
FIT IN THE SPACE OF A STAMP

PHONE WIRES
SERIES WIRED
PARALLEL WIRED
ANTENNA

A PHONE BUG CAN BE
AS SMALL AS A PEA

SLOTS IN SCREWS LEFT AT 45 DEG ANGLE
TO TELL IF THEY HAVE BEEN REMOVED

RCA

SCREW PAINTED WITH CHEMICAL THAT
GLOWS UNDER ULTRAVIOLET LIGHT

SCREW PAINTED OVER WITH TWO
COLORS OF NAIL POLISH

METAL SHIELD
FREQ ADJUST
MIC
MADE IN USA
AA CELL

WIRELESS MICROPHONE BUG
(ACTUAL SIZE)

"WINDOW"

'SIDEBANDS'

'BLIP' ON SCREEN OF A
SPECTRUM ANALYZER

SHAPE SHOWS MODE; AM,FM...
HEIGHT SHOWS SIGNAL STRENGTH

ORGANIC BUG
(ACTUAL SIZE)

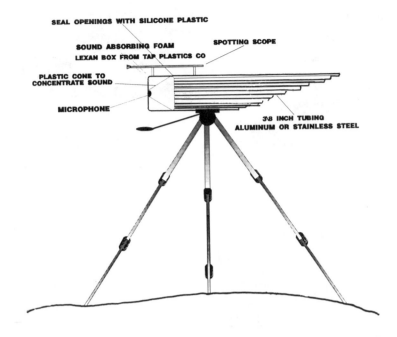

'GATLING' TYPE
SHOTGUN MICROPHONE

OPTOELECTRONICS

R10 COMMUNICATIONS TEST RECEIVER
Introductory Price $299.

The *NEW* OPTOELECTRONICS R10 is a self contained FM modulation monitor that will lock on and demodulate signals from nearby transmitters. It can be used to check the modulation quality of most land mobile transmitters and with the use of a frequency counter can be used to verify many signalling tones including CTCSS and DTMF. The R10 is easy to use and provides a fast, inexpensive alternative to service monitors to verify transmitter modulation.

OPTIONS
NiCad 90
Rechargeable NiCad Battery ....$75.
TA100
Telescoping Whip Antenna with swivel base for bench/field use. ....$14.

Order Today!
Optoelectronics, Inc.
5821 Northeast 14th Avenue
Fort Lauderdale, Florida 33334
Toll Free Order Line: 1-800-327-5912
In FL: 305-771-2050 • FAX: 305-771-2052

PRELIMINARY SPECIFICATIONS

Frequency Range	30-1000MHz
Demodulation	FM
Deviation Range	up to 50kHz
Frequency Response	50 - 5000Hz
Auto Tune Time	less than 2 seconds
Input	50Ω, approximately 0 dBm
Outputs	Front panel Speaker, Front panel Audio out
Front Panel Controls	Audio Level, Squelch, Power
Front Panel Indicators	Lock, Power, Low Battery
Power Requirements	9 VDC 200mA
Rear Panel Output	Output for model PC10 (PC based multi function counter) permits high resolution reciprocal measurements and data logging.
Compact Aluminum Cabinet	3.5"H. x 7.3" W. x 6.8" D. Textured Polycarbonate/ Aluminum laminate front and rear panels.

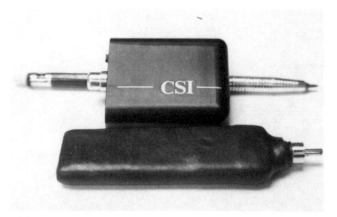

CSI tape-recorder detector.

The Hunter from CSI.

CSI phone-tap detector.

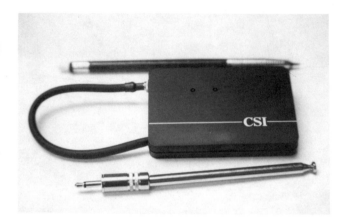

The Informer bug detector from CSI.

The "Exterminator" ultrasonic sound microphone jammer.

APPENDIX C

LIST OF SUPPLIERS

The asterisk (*) after some companies indicates that all requests should be sent on a company letterhead. These companies deal only with established businesses or government agencies.

Unless otherwise stated, I believe (or know from personal experience) all of the products listed here to be of good quality, or I wouldn't have included them. I have neither asked for, received, nor been offered any form of compensation from any business in exchange for listing them. I plug 'em as I see 'em.

2600
P.O. Box 752
Middle Island, NY 11953

2600 takes its name from the old 2,600-cycle tone that was used by the original "boxers," such as Captain Crunch, to get free long-distance calls from Ma Bell. 2600 contains interesting information about telco, such as the latest ANI and CNA numbers, and much more. The original phreakers' publication. After all these years, it's still around.

Alpha Industries, Inc. *
651 Lowell Avenue
Methuen, MA 01844

Radio frequency (microwave) surveillance systems built to military specifications.

Amazing Concepts
P.O. Box 716
Amherst, NH 03031

Sells kits for FM transmitters and phone bugs.

Also known as Information Unlimited, which has Tesla coil kits and plasma generators and other interesting stuff. Free catalog.

American Laser Systems *
106 Fowler Road
Goleta, CA 93117

Optical surveillance systems built to military specifications.

Antenna Specialists
30500 Bruce Industrial Highway
Cleveland, OH 44139

Antennas, all kinds of antennas.

Bit Connection
719 S. Harbor Boulevard
Fullerton, CA 92632

The Bit Connection has those sometimes hard-to-find TORX bits that open the "security screws" that are on some telco blocks and SPSP connectors. A set of four popular sizes is $12.95, shipped COD.

Buttonware
P.O. Box 5786
Bellevue, WA 98006

Computer shareware.

Capri Electronics Corporation
P.O. Box 589
Bayfield, CO 81122

"Privacy assurance" devices. Equipment for

detecting bugs, wireless microphones, and video cameras, among other things. It also has telephone accessories and books. Its TD-53 bug detector has accessory probes for locating the light modulator and infrared bugs and lasers described in the text.

I tested the TD-53. A low-power wireless microphone was hidden inside a retail store while I waited outside (and didn't peek), and I found it in less than a minute. It also has the verify feature. Capri's equipment is moderately priced, and its people are friendly and helpful. I was impressed and recommend Capri.

C&S Sales, Inc.
1245 Rosewood
Deerfield, IL 60015

Test equipment, function generators, and a breadboard minilab for building small electronic projects such as wireless mics with a built-in power supply and wave generators. In kit form, it is $119.95, or $139.95 assembled. Seems like a good deal to me.

CBC International
P.O. Box 31500
Phoenix, AZ 85046

CBC has technical information on modifying CB radios and scanners and building linear amplifiers, and it also carries a large selection of books. Many of its books are very good, but some are a little overpriced. The one on modifying scanners, for example, has a little info on the subject, and the rest is padded with stuff that, while useful, is in some of CBI's other books.

Cony Manufacturing
Room 301, Hirooka Building
#59, 2 Chome
Kangetsu cho
Chikusa-Ku Nagoya 464
JAPAN

Cony manufactures a variety of variable-frequency transmitters and wireless microphones, some of which are sold in spy shops such as the Spy Factory. Depending on whom you ask, they either do or do not export to the United States. I wrote to them eons ago, but I have not yet received a reply.

Consumertronics
2011 Crescent Drive
P.O. Drawer 537
Alamogordo, NM 88310

Consumertronics sells, among other things, plans for building the van Eck computer-eavesdropping system. I sent for them, and for $37 (including UPS, COD), I received a 14-page manual that, for the price, could have been better presented and of better quality. I have not built it, so I do not know if it works or not.

It also has "stealth paints" that will "shield a vehicle from any type of radar detection," "resonant coils that gather high-intensity, harmful electrical noise from the unseen but omnipresent electrosphere and repackage it as pure and precise harmonic energy," and a "laying-on-of-hands amplifier, cerebral synchronizer, and ESP communicator." I have been meaning to buy an ESP communicator for a long time, but I didn't know where to get one.

If these work, then the van Eck circuit probably does also.

Countersurveillance Systems, Inc. (CSI)
1203 Normandy Way
Santa Clara, CA 90500

CSI, located in the heart of smoggy Silicon Valley, makes The Hunter described in the text, bug and tape-recorder detectors, an ultrasonic sound microphone jammer (The Exterminator), and a four-foot parabolic microphone, among other things. Its products are nicely made and professionally packaged, as you can see in Appendix B.

Deco Industries
Box 607
Bedford Hills, NY 10507

Deco has kits for miniature FM transmitters, phone bugs, etc. It has recently contracted with a company that manufactures integrated circuits for a custom-made chip that is the heart of its new wireless microphone kit.

This is the model VT-75, which has a power output of from 75 to 100 milliwatts, depending on the battery voltage, which can be from 6 to 12 volts. Many wireless microphones, some of which cost four times as much, have an output of less than one-fourth as much as the VT-75. It is 9/16 by 1 1/4 inches, and the frequency can be adjusted with a screwdriver, and with a wire antenna only 12 inches long, it has a range of several blocks or more. The VT-75 is in kit form. You have to attach the microphone and antenna wire. Retail price is about $50, and it's the best deal around.

Deco also has a long-play microcassette recorder and several phone bug kits. Write for a free catalog.

Dektor Counter Intelligence & Security*
515 Barnhard Street
Savannah, GA 31401

Offers professional countermeasures services to the private sector, conducts classes and seminars on the subject, and markets a complete line of countermeasures equipment both to the public and law enforcement. Serious inquiries, please.

Eden Press
P.O. Box 8410
Fountain Valley, CA 92728

Eden Press is well-known for its books on privacy and the right to be left alone by government snoops. It has published the classic works on paper tripping and has a wide variety of books on other subjects such as how to hide things, secret agent stuff, financial privacy, offshore banking, Swiss banks, and many nifty ways to make money. Other books are on disguises, revenge, and much, much more. Eden's catalogue is free and highly recommended.

Edmund Scientific, Inc.
101 E. Gloucester Pike
Barrington, NJ 08007

Edmund Scientific is an old established company with a well-deserved reputation for quality products for scientists, students of science, hobbyists, and experimenters. Its colorful 187-page catalogue has a vast selection of fascinating products. It specializes in optics and has page after page of lenses, mirrors, microscopes, lasers, accessories, fiberoptics, borescopes, telescopes, binoculars, filters, infrared and ultraviolet light sources, zillions of magnets, lab equipment and supplies, educational aids and kits, and a whole lot more.This is one of the most fascinating catalogs around.

Electronic Equipment Bank, Inc. (EEB)
516 Mill Street, NE
Vienna, VA 22180

EEB has one of the largest selections of communications receivers and scanners I know of, which includes Sony, Realistic, Japan Radio, Kenwood, Yaesu, Panasonic, Bearcat, Sangean, Drake, and Icom (my favorite).

EEB has the not-so-easy-to-find Fairmate HP200 1,000-channel portable scanner, the AR-3000, which is one helluva scanner even if it isn't made by Icom; a nice selection of books, antennas, and accessories; and the affordable AX-700 spectrum analyzer mentioned in the text.

Electronic Rainbow, Inc.
6254 LaPas Trail
Indianapolis, IN 46268

The Rainbow has kits for building wireless microphones, phone bugs, a high-gain amplifier that can be used with a parabolic microphone, or as a listen-down-the-line amplifier. For $15, Rainbow sells a book with the schematics and circuit board layout, instructions, and parts list for these and ten other kits. This is a good deal, I think.

Electro-Space Systems*
P.O. Box 831359
Richardson, TX 75083

Military optical surveillance systems.

Elenco Electronics
150 W. Carpenter Avenue
Wheeling, IL 60090

Elenco has a nice selection of electronic test equipment, tools, soldering irons, power supplies, function generators, and breadboards for designing electronic things. It also has kits for building wireless microphones and phone bugs and a sound-activated relay, which can have some interesting applications if you think about it.

Everett Enterprises
7855 Wintercress Dr.
Springfield, VA 2f2152

Private-line DES programs for computers.

Excalibur Enterprises
P.O. Box 266
Emmans, PA 18049

Night-vision stuff and starlight scopes for spying on spies.

Full Disclosure
P.O. Box 903
Libertyville, IL 60048

Full Disclosure is a small (volume 23 is 16 pages) newspaper that has up-to-date information on electronic surveillance methods and equipment, interesting articles, and classified ads. The latest issue has articles on fax interception, the alleged FCC attempt to intimidate companies that sell kits and wireless microphones, and some other stuff on what the feds are up to, such as bids to buy surveillance equipment (e.g., the FBI wants to buy Panasonic RN-36 microcassette recorders, and the DEA wants to rent an antenna site from WCIX-TV in Miami). I like this interesting publication. Twelve issues per year for $18.

Grove Enterprises
140 Dog Branch Road
P.O. Box 98
Brasstown, NC 28902

Grove has communications receivers, scanners, and accessories, and it sells the excellent AR-3000 that I keep plugging.

Halted Specialties Co.
3500 Ryder St.
Santa Clara, CA 95051

Halted is a large retail store that has communications receivers and ham equipment, parts and test equipment, computers, and all that, but what is the most interesting is its large selection of used and surplus gear. It also has lasers (usually inexpensive) and other optical goodies that are useful in spying on spies. You can spend hours browsing through the many aisles of stuff.

Heath Company
Benton Harbor, MI 49022

Heath has been around for close to 50 years and has a large line of communications, test equipment and ham gear, and consumer goodies useful in se-curing your home from spies. It has infrared motion detectors, the Radar Watchdog that detects motion through walls, portable alarms that are activated by opening a door, closed-circuit television cameras, and many other nifty things. Much of its electronic gear is available in the form of kits, and over the years, I have built a number of them. All were of excellent quality and easy to build. I like Heath.

Intelligence Group
1628 Lombard Street
San Francisco, CA 94118

The Intelligence Group is a deceptively small, modernistic store with pretty neon signs and fascinating display cases. In one is a realistic copy of a Smith & Wesson 9mm automatic with attached laser sight (real), a Cobra electronic lockpick that the owner of the store invented, and a collection of authentic police department badges. In another is The Hunter, a spectrum analyzer, the CPM-700 surveillance monitor, and other goodies. It also has scanners, stun guns, and a large selection of books, including Lee Lapin's new one, *Book II, How to Get Anything on Anybody*.

This is what you see in the store. You don't see the closed-circuit cameras that are hidden in some things in which you wouldn't expect to find them, or the complete electronics lab and machine shop in the back, where the company makes its own TV cameras and other equipment. It's not open to the public, though.

IG also does professional countersurveillance sweeps. Stop in when you are in San Francisco. It's just a few blocks west of Van Ness Avenue (U.S. 101).

International Logistics Systems, Inc.*
P.O. Box 25-T
295 Courtlandt Street
Belleville, NJ 07109

This company carries police, security, and executive-protection equipment, including bomb detection and countersurveillance gear. Serious inquiries.

Interphase International, Ltd. *
15650-A Vinyard, Suite 115
Morgan Hill, CA 95037

Interphase is the distributor of the ultrasmall TV camera with the built-in transmitter described in the text. It sells mainly to law-enforcement and security companies, and it doesn't mail catalogs.

Jameco Electronics
1355 Shoreway Road
Belmont, CA 94002

A large and impressive collection of computers, test equipment, parts, tools, cabinets and enclosures, power supplies, cables and connectors, integrated circuits, breadboards and books. Nice color catalogs are free. Stop in if you are in the area.

Litton Applied Technology *
645 Almanor Avenue
Sunnyvale, CA 94088

Military microwave surveillance equipment.

LNR Communications, Inc. *
180 Marcus Boulevard
Hauppauge, NY 11788

Microwave receivers.

Loompanics Unlimited
P.O. Box 1197
Port Townsend, WA 98368

Loompanics describes itself on the front page of its 230-page catalog as "Sellers of Unusual Books." A bit of an understatement, I'd say. Loompanics lists hundreds of books on subjects that you won't find at B. Dalton, such as the underground economy, privacy (your friend and mine), Big Brother, frauds and cons, guerrilla warfare, knives, guns, bombs, anarchy, alternative living, and much more. It also has interesting articles and even cartoons.

If you are interested in just about anything besides working 9 to 5 for someone else and spending the rest of your time being brainwashed by the boob tube, then you will find something useful in the Loompanics catalog. It used to be free, but now it is $3 and is well worth the price. Highly recommended.

Micro-Tel Division *
Adams-Russell Co.
10713 Gilroy Road
Hunt Valley, MD 21030

Microwave surveillance systems.

Microwave Systems, Inc. *
6075 E. Molloy Road
Syracuse, NY 13211

Microwave receivers.

Mobile Radio Resources
1224 Madrona Avenue
San Jose, CA 95125

MRR has two books of interest to scanner enthusiasts. The first is *Government Radio Systems*, which covers California, and put simply, "It's the only book you need."

The local government issue is 448 pages and has the frequencies of virtually every city, county, and state government agency that exists. It goes beyond just lists of numbers, as it includes repeater input frequencies and tone-squelch codes, locations of repeater systems, and channel numbers and how they are assigned. For example, in Los Angeles County there are no fewer than 14 pages devoted to local police, from the Long Beach area to Arcadia, which include primary and secondary channels, links to other departments, detective and narcotics team frequencies, traffic divisions, separate listings for the various precincts in Los Angeles, such as Central, Rampart, Valley, etc. The federal government version is just as complete and lists about every agency in California, including DEA, FBI, Secret Service, INS, Customs, and others. The Secret Service listings, for example, include frequencies assigned to the vice president protection detail, the Night Hawk and Marine One helicopters and Air Force One, White House security, Capitol Police, and more.

The second book is *Military Radio Systems* by Bob Kelty. This one you've got to see. I have known Bob for years and can tell you that there aren't many people who know as much about scanners and radio frequencies as he does.

Nuts and Volts Magazine
P.O. Box 1639
Placentia, CA 92670

Nuts and Volts is a 100-plus-page catalog (April 1991 issue) that has both personal and commercial ads for almost anything that a hobbyist could want. Surplus electronic and test equipment, ham radio gear, parts kits, computer hard- and software, satellite TV decoders, solar cell panels (for powering shotgun microphone amplifiers and other antispy goodies), tools, books, and hard-to-find manuals for old equipment.

It has classified ad sections for information wanted, things for sale or trade, and a calendar of events such as electronic flea markets and the like. *Nuts and Volts* is an excellent source of information. A subscription is $15 per year (12 issues), and a free sample copy is available on request.

Optoelectronics
5821 NE 14th Avenue
Ft. Lauderdale, FL 33334

Optoelectronics makes frequency counters as described in the text. It has various portable models that range from 10 cycles to 2.6 gc. and from $179 to $379, as well as lab-quality bench models. It also makes a circuit board that plugs into a personal computer, which makes it into a frequency counter with the frequency displayed on the monitor screen. It runs under Microsoft Windows 3.0.

Another fascinating product Optoelectronics makes is the R-10, which is a communications test receiver that receives and also demodulates signals from nearby transmitters, such as bugs. The demodulator separates the sound from the signal carrier, which means you can hear what is being transmitted, just as in the verify mode of the TD-53 bug detector. You remember that from the text, right? It covers 30 to 1,000 mc. and presently is 3.5 x 7.3 x 6.8 inches, but the company will soon market it in the same size as its pocket-size counters.

The most interesting product Optoelectronics sells is the model APS204R1 preselector. This little goodie increases the sensitivity of the model 3000 counter pictured in Appendix B so that it picks up a cellular phone from 250 feet away. Fascinating.

Paladin Press
P.O. Box 1307
Boulder, CO 80306

Paladin has a large selection of books on many subjects. It specializes in weapons, self-defense, the martial arts, military science, and survival, and has an impressive selection that includes some interesting titles on knives, such as *The Complete Bladesmith* and *The Master Bladesmith* on making them. Paladin also has titles on getting even, paper tripping, credit, secret hiding places, anarchy, con games, and, of course, electronic surveillance and countersurveillance—including both *How to Get Anything on Anybody* books by Lee Lapin and this book, of course. Its catalog, which is highly recommended, also frequently includes interviews with some of its authors.

PK Elektronik
Heidenkampschweig 74
200 Hamburg 1
Federal Republik of Germany

PK makes both surveillance and counter surveillance gear. The factory is in Germany, but the company has a sales office in New York. (I didn't know that until I called the factory. "Kann ich ein katalog haben, bitte, fur mein book ich bein gerschriben?" I tried to ask before he said, "I speak English.") He told me that the company does not export to private citizens in the United States, only to law-enforcement agencies, the same as the New York sales office. However, it does sell to people who live in Germany (and some other countries), so if sie haben ein freund im Deutschland. He said he would send a catalog, but I haven't received it yet.

Reality Check
(415) 567-7043
1200-2400 BAUD N81

Formerly Just Say Yes, Reality Check is a computer-bulletin board that has current information on what telco is up to. Some of it is quite technical, but some is understandable to beginners. This is a "handle" BBS; it doesn't dig into your personal life or ask a lot of questions to give you access. It is not a pirate BBS, but it has a lot of useful data if you are into telco information.

RSA Data Security, Inc.
10 Twin Dolphin Dr.
Redwood, CA 94065

MailSafe public key program.

Scanners Unlimited
San Carlos, CA

Scanners Unlimited is located a few miles south of San Francisco, and it has a nice selection of scanning radios, which includes Uniden and Realistic, and lots of accessories, books, antennas, etc. I bought my PRO-2006 there.

Scanner World, USA
10 New Scotland Avenue
Albany, NY 12208

Scanner World has been around for as long as scanners have. It has a wide variety of scanners, CB radios, antennas, and accessories. Its catalog is free for the asking.

Sherwood Communications Associates
P.O. Box 535-A
Southampton, PA 18966

Remember the three monkeys, "See no evil, hear no evil, speak no evil"? The first thing I noticed when I got this catalog was the logo, which is a drawing of three heads (human rather than primate). The first has a night-vision device, the second has a microphone, and the third is wearing headphones. I got a kick out of that even though it was probably not designed with levity in mind.

Sherwood is big on video. It has one closed-circuit camera that is the size of a cigarette pack (remember those?) and another that is on an unenclosed printed circuit board using the new surface-mount technology made to conceal inside a smoke detector, complete with wide-angle lens; pinhole lenses that can peek through a tiny hole, and even one that is disguised as a sprinkler head; and a briefcase with camera and VCR inside and small transmitters that send the camera's signal 3,500 feet.

Besides video equipment, Sherwood has directional microphones, telephone accessories (lots of these), tape recorders, two-way radio equipment (including a portable repeater), telephone scramblers, voice-alteration devices, document shredders, night-vision equipment, and the list goes on.

What I find most fascinating is the line of vehicle-surveillance equipment—everything you need to set up a van for spying. The line includes a periscope disguised as an air vent, a swivel chair for 360-degree viewing, camera lenses disguised as reflectors, a silent air conditioner, a bunk bed with storage area, and even a chemical toilet for long-term surveillance.

When I first talked to the people at Sherwood, they said the catalog is "an education in itself." I agree. Sherwood's catalog is 40 pages with lots of illustrations and a nice book list. It costs $10 and is well worth it.

Spy Factory, Inc.
500 Beach Street
San Francisco, CA 94113

Spy Factory is located at Fisherman's Wharf in the Anchorage shopping center. It is one of a chain of eleven stores with the head offices in San Antonio.

It has a variety of interesting products for sale, including several models of bug detectors and other countersurveillance devices, wireless microphones from different manufacturers, invisible marking chemicals that glow under ultraviolet light, stun guns, telephone scramblers, and a large assortment of those clever hiding devices made from the containers of common household products. Just unscrew the top, or maybe the bottom, and stash your goodies inside. A burglar will think they are real because they are.

The salespeople are friendly and willing to demonstrate their products as time permits. Other shops are in Dallas, El Paso, Houston, Tucson, San Diego, Las Vegas, Costa Mesa, West Hollywood, and Sacramento.

Super Software
403 E. Nasa Rd.
Webster, TX 77598

DES computer programs.

SWS Security*
1300 Boyd Road
Street, MD 21154

Electronic surveillance and communications equipment for government and private agencies.

Tucker Surplus Store
1801 Reserve Street
Garland, TX 75355

Tucker's latest catalog is 53 pages, with lots of surplus electronic equipment and reasonable prices. It has meters for measuring phone line resistance and voltage, a reflectometer or two, function generators that—with an antenna and maybe a one-transistor amplifier—will jam a van Eck computer snooper system, and lots of other stuff, including a low-cost spectrum analyzer, just in case you have no budget for the $80,000 Hewlett-Packard model.

Viking International
150 Executive Park Boulevard
San Francisco, CA 94134

Viking has some excellent audio equipment such as long-play tape recorders, specialized microphones and preamplifiers, dropout relays, and "The Firefly," a small battery-powered infrared light source that can be carried around in the field to make it easier to tell the good guys from the bad guys, or the other way around. Its long-play recorders are not the cheapo types that have a resistor connected across the remote-control jack; they have special electronic circuits to compensate for the extended recording time, which improves the audio quality.

ZK Celltest Systems*
137 E. Fremont Avenue
Sunnyvale, CA 94087

ZK makes a pocket-size SAM, which you remember is a cellular radio system access monitor. On its front panel, it displays the numbers from the NAM of a cellular phone from its radio signal and stores them for later printing. ZK is picky about whom it will sell to; it won't sell one to just anyone who wants one.

APPENDIX D
FREQUENCY LIST

The following frequencies are likely to be used for bugs.

CITIZENS BAND CHANNELS 01 TO 40

01: 26.965 mc.	21: 27.215 mc.
02: 26.975 mc.	22: 27.225 mc.
03: 26.985 mc.	23: 27.235 mc.
04: 27.005 mc.	24: 27.245 mc.
05: 27.015 mc.	25: 27.255 mc.
06: 27.025 mc.	26: 27.265 mc.
07: 27.035 mc.	27: 27.275 mc.
08: 27.055 mc.	28: 27.285 mc.
09: 27.065 mc.	29: 27.295 mc.
10: 27.075 mc.	30: 27.305 mc.
11: 27.085 mc.	31: 27.315 mc.
12: 27.105 mc.	32: 27.325 mc.
13: 27.115 mc.	33: 27.335 mc.
14: 27.125 mc.	34: 27.345 mc.
15: 27.135 mc.	35: 27.355 mc.
16: 27.155 mc.	36: 27.365 mc.
17: 27.165 mc.	37: 27.375 mc.
18: 27.175 mc.	38: 27.385 mc.
19: 27.185 mc.	39: 27.395 mc.
20: 27.205 mc.	40: 27.405 mc.

AUDIO FREQUENCIES FOR TV BROADCASTING CHANNELS 02 TO 69

59.75 mc.	TV ch. 2
65.75 mc.	TV ch. 3
71.75 mc.	TV ch. 4
81.75 mc.	TV ch. 5
87.75 mc.	TV ch. 6
179.75 mc.	TV ch. 7
185.75 mc.	TV ch. 8
191.75 mc.	TV ch. 9
197.75 mc.	TV ch. 10
203.75 mc.	TV ch. 11
209.75 mc.	TV ch. 12
215.75 mc.	TV ch. 13
475.75 mc.	TV ch. 14
481.75 mc.	TV ch. 15

In the snuggling method described in the text, a bug will transmit close to one of these frequencies, usually the lower channels 2 to 5. A bug made from the Motorola MC2833 chip works only on channel 2, as its highest effective frequency is 60 mc.

OLD CORDLESS TELEPHONE FREQUENCIES

Base	Mobile
1.705 mc.	49.67 mc.
1.735 mc.	49.845 mc.
1.765 mc.	49.86 mc.
1.795 mc.	49.77 mc.
1.825 mc.	49.875 mc.

NEW CORDLESS TELEPHONE FREQUENCIES

46.61 mc.	49.67 mc.
46.63 mc.	49.845 mc.
46.67 mc.	49.86 mc.
46.71 mc.	49.77 mc.
46.73 mc.	49.875 mc.
46.77 mc.	49.83 mc.
46.83 mc.	49.89 mc.
46.87 mc.	49.93 mc.
46.93 mc.	49.99 mc.
46.97 mc.	49.97 mc.

WIRELESS MICROPHONES

36.70, 37.10, 37.16, 40.68, 42.89, 44.87, 47.27, 169.45, 169.505, 170.245, 170.045, 171.105, 171.845, 171.905

UNKNOWN

Conversations have been reported on the following frequencies.

47.42, 47.46, 47.50, 49.375, 49.39, 49.405, 49.42, 49.435, 49.70, 49.80

FAST-FOOD RESTAURANT DRIVE-UP WINDOWS

McDonald's	35.020	and	154.600
	30.840	and	154.570
	33.140	and	151.895
Burgerville	30.840	and	154.570
?	?	and	157.595

Burger King	467.825	and	457.600
Taco Bell	460.8875		
Hardee's	030.84	and	154.57
?	031.000	and	170.305
?	154.600	and	171.105
?	170.245	and	154.570

WIRELESS BABY MONITORS
(use cordless phone frequencies)

49.83 49.845 49.86 49.875 49.89

AUDITORY AIDS FOR HEARING IMPAIRED

72.025 to 72.975 and 75.475 to 75.975

These are a small transmitter/receiver set. The receiver is used like a hearing aid, and the transmitter can be beside a telephone doorbell, the speaker in a lecture hall, etc.

FEDERAL FREQUENCIES

The following frequency areas are listed as being used by undercover federal agents. Since they have been published, they have probably been changed, but one never knows. These are from Bob Kelty's book.

FBI

Mobile Tracking "Bumper Beepers"

40.170	40.220

Wireless Microphones

169.445	169.505	170.245	170.305
171.045	171.105	171.845	171.905

Body Taps or Wires

171.450	171.600	171.750	171.850
172.000	172.2125	172.2375	172.2625
172.2875	172.3125	172.3375	172.3625
172.3875			

DEA

418.750   418.675

SECRET SERVICE

407.800   406.275   408.500   408.975

TREASURY DEPARTMENT/BUREAU OF ALCOHOL, TOBACCO, AND FIREARMS

166.2875   170.4125

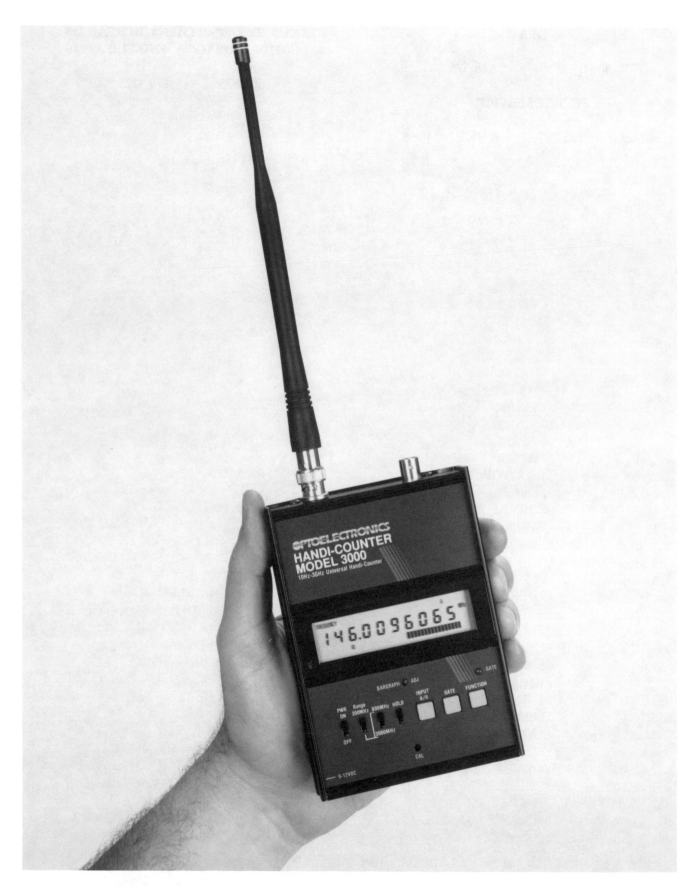

APPENDIX E

FREQUENCY ALLOCATION TABLE

029.000-029.800	FOREST PRODUCTS	039.020-039.980	POLICE LOCAL GOVT.
029.800-029.890	FIXED SERVICE	040.000-042.000	FEDERAL GOVT.
029.900-029.910	FEDERAL GOVT.	042.020-042.940	STATE POLICE
029.920-029.990	FIXED SERVICE	042.960-043.000	BUSINESS
030.000-030.560	FEDERAL GOVT.	043.020-043.180	SPECIAL INDUSTRIAL
030.560-030.660	SPECIAL INDUSTRIAL	043.180-043.220	TELEPHONE MAINT.
030.660-030.820	PETROL-FOREST-TRUCKING	043.220-043.620	MOBILE PHONE PAGING
030.840-031.260	BUSINESS TRUCKING		INDUSTRIAL
	FORESTRY	043.640-043.680	MOBILE PHONE EMERGENCY
031.280-031.980	FORESTRY CONSERVATION		PAGING
	INDUSTRIAL	043.700-044.600	TRUCKING
032.000-033.000	FEDERAL GOVT.	044.620-045.040	POLICE FORESTRY
033.020-033.160	HIWAY MAINT. SPEC. EMERG.	045.060-045.640	POLICE LOCAL GOVT.
	BUSINESS	045.660-045.860	POLICE HIWAY MAINT.
033.180-033.380	PETROLEUM RADIO SERVICE	045.880-045.890	FIRE INTERSYSTEM NET
033.380-033.420	BUSINESS	045.900-046.040	POLICE SPECIAL EMERG.
033.420-033.980	FIRE	046.040-046.500	FIRE
034.000-035.000	FEDERAL GOVT.	046.520-046.580	LOCAL GOVT.
035.020-035.180	BUSINESS	046.600-047.000	FEDERAL GOVT.
035.160-035.220	TELEPHONE MAINT.	047.020-047.400	HIWAY MAINT.
035.220-035.620	MOBILE PHONE PAGING	047.420-047.680	SPECIAL EMERG.,
035.640-035.680	MOBILE PHONE EMERGENCY		INDUSTRIAL
	PAGING	047.700-048.540	POWER COMPANIES
035.700-035.720	BUSINESS	048.560-049.500	FOREST PRODUCTS, PETROL
035.740-035.860	SPECIAL INDUSTRIAL	049.520-049.580	FOREST PRODUCTS, PETROL
035.880-035.980	BUSINESS	049.600-050.000	FEDERAL GOVT.
036.000-037.000	FEDERAL GOVT.	050.000-054.000	HAM SIX METERS
037.020-037.420	POLICE LOCAL GOVT.	054.000-072.000	TV CHANNELS 2, 3, 4
037.420-037.460	FOREST PRODUCTS	072.000-076.000	FIXED, PORTABLE
037.460-037.860	POWER COMPANIES	076.000-088.000	TV CHANNELS 5, 6
037.860-037.900	FOREST PRODUCTS	088.000-108.000	FM BROADCASTING
037.900-037.980	HIWAY MAINT.	108.000-117.950	AERO, NAVIGATION
038.000-039.000	FEDERAL GOVT.	118.000-128.800	AERO, AIR-TRAFFIC CONTROL

128.825-132.000	AERO, AIRLINE FREQUENCIES
132.000-136.000	AERO, AIR-TRAFFIC CONTROL
136.000-144.000	FEDERAL GOVT.
144.000-148.000	HAM TWO METERS
148.000-150.800	FEDERAL GOVT.
150.815-150.965	AUTO CLUBS, TOW TRUCKS
150.965-150.995	PETROL, OIL SPILL CLEAN-UP
150.995-151.130	HIWAY MAINT.
151.145-151.490	FORESTRY CONSERVATION
151.490-151.595	SPECIAL INDUSTRIAL
151.625-151.955	BUSINESS
151.985-152.065	TELEPHONE MAINT.
152.075-152.125	EMERGENCY PAGING
152.130-152.240	RCC
152.270-152.480	TAXI BUSINESS
152.510-152.810	MOBILE PHONE
152.840-152.860	PAGING
152.870-153.035	REMOTE BROADCAST, MOVIE COMPANIES
153.035-153.395	REMOTE PICKUP FOREST PRODUCTS
153.410-153.725	POWER COMPANIES
153.740-154.115	FIRE, LOCAL GOVT.
153.130-154.445	FIRE
154.460-154.490	LOCAL GOVT. POWER SPECIAL INDUSTRIAL
154.515-154.575	BUSINESS FOREST PRODUCTS
154.585-154-640	PETROL, OIL SPILL CLEAN-UP
154.650-154.950	POLICE (USUALLY COUNTY AND STATE)
154.965-155.145	POLICE LOCAL GOVT.
155.160-155.400	POLICE, SPECIAL EMERGENCY
155.415-155.700	POLICE
155.715-156.030	POLICE, LOCAL GOVT.
156.045-156.240	HIWAY MAINT., POLICE
156.275-157.425	MARINE
157.425-157.470	PAGING
157.450	EMERGENCY PAGING
157.470-157.515	AUTO EMERG. SERV., AUTO CLUBS, TOWING
157.530-157.710	TAXI
157.740-157.760	PAGING
157.770-158.070	MOBILE PHONE (MOBILE UNITS)
158.200	PAGING
158.130-158.265	POWER, PETROL
158.280-158.460	PETROL, FOREST
158.490-158.670	RCC MOBILE UNITS
158.700	PAGING
158.730-158.970	POLICE, LOCAL GOVT.
158.985-159.195	POLICE, HIWAY MAINT.
159.225-159.465	FOREST CONSERVATION
159.470-157.490	PETROL OILSPILL CLEAN-UP
159.495-160.200	TRUCKING
160.215-161.565	RAILROAD
161.600	MARINE
161.640-161.760	REMOTE PICKUP
161.800-162.000	MARINE PHONE
162.000-174.000	FEDERAL GOVT.
163.250	EMERGENCY PAGING
166.250	REMOTE PICKUP
170.150	REMOTE PICKUP
173.225-173.375	RELAY PRESS, NEWSPAPERS, FOREST, PETROL
174.000-216.000	TV CH 7-13
216.000-220.000	FEDERAL GOVT., TELEMETRY
220.000-225.000	HAM
225.000-400.000	FEDERAL GOVT., MILITARY AIRCRAFT
400.000-406.100	SATELLITE, METEROLOGICAL
406.000-420.000	FEDERAL GOVT.
420.000-450.000	HAM
450.000-451.000	REMOTE PICKUP
451.025-451.150	POWER
451.175-451.750	POWER PETROL FOREST
451.775-452.025	SPECIAL INDUSTRIAL
452.050-452.300	TAXI FOREST PRODUCTS
452.325-452.500	TAXI, FOREST PRODUCTS, TRUCKING, RAILROAD
452.525-452.600	AUTO CLUB, TOWING
452.625-452.950	TRUCKING, RAILROAD
452.975-453.000	RELAY PRESS, NEWSPAPERS
453.025-453.975	POLICE LOCAL GOVT. HIWAY MAINT. FIRE
454.000	PETROL OIL SPILL CLEAN-UP
454.025-454.350	RCC
454.375-454.975	MOBILE PHONE
455.000-456.000	REMOTE PICKUP
456.000-460.000	MOBILE REPEATER UNITS 5 MC. ABOVE REPEATER
460.025-460.550	POLICE REPEATER OUTPUT
460.575-460.625	FIRE REPEATER OUTPUT
460.650-462.175	BUSINESS TRUCKING TAXI
462.200-462.450	MANUFACTURERS
462.475-462.525	MFG. POWER TELEPHONE MAINT. FOREST PROD.

462.550-462.725	GENERAL MOBILE RADIO SERVICE (CB)
462.750-462.925	BUSINESS PAGING
462.950-463.175	SPECIAL EMERGENCY
463.200-465.000	BUSINESS
456.000-470.000	MOBILE UNITS 5 MC. ABOVE REPEATER OUT
470.000-806.000	TV UHF
806.000-809.750	MOBILE PHONE
809.750-816.000	TRUNKED MOBILE PHONE
816.000-821.000	TRUNKED MOBILE PHONE
821.000-825.000	PHONE SATELLITE UPLINK
825.000-835.000	CELULLAR, MOBILE UNITS, NONWIRE
835.000-845.000	CELULLAR, MOBILE UNITS, WIRE
845.000-851.000	CELLULAR CONTROL CHANNELS
851.000-854.750	MOBILE PHONE BASE
854.750-861.000	MOBILE PHONE
861.000-866.000	MOBILE PHONE BASE UNITS
866.000-870.000	PHONE SATELLITE DOWNLINK
870.000-880.000	CELLULAR PHONE BASE, NONWIRE
880.000-890.000	CELLULAR PHONE BASE, WIRE
890.000-896.000	CELLULAR CONTROL CHANNELS
896.000-902.000	PRIVATE BUSINESS RADIO

EXPLANATION OF TERMS AND USEFUL INFORMATION

SPECIAL ENERGENCY: This can be anything from private or police search and rescue to ambulance companies to disaster relief organizations (Red Cross) and can even be beach patrols or school buses.

FIXED SERVICE: These frequencies can be used by any service, both private and government, and are for base-to-base only, no mobiles.

GMRS: This is the General Mobile Radio Service, the "UHF Citizens Band."

FIXED-PORTABLE: For base stations that have portable (hand-held) units not installed in vehicles.

RCC: Radio Common Carrier. These frequencies are assigned to private businesses for mobile telephone (not cellular) use and other uses.

LOCAL GOVERNMENT: This is usually for city or county agencies such as the street maintenance crews, water company, public library security, and the security guards at colleges and universities.

For further details, see the CFR (Code of Federal Regulations) Part II. These books are in all public libraries.

APPENDIX F

HOW CELLULAR RADIOS WORK

WARNING: Monitoring cellular radio frequencies is a violation of federal law, the Electronics Communications Privacy Act of 1986.

The following is for informational purposes only and is intended to reveal not how easily cellular radio can be monitored, which has been widely publicized, but that it is possible to track a particular conversation with a very high degree of success, which has not been well-publicized.

There are people who don't want you to know this.

The frequencies used by the cellular-phone system are public domain information—available to anyone. However, to track a given conversation, it is also necessary to know the frequencies used by the individual cells, known as "sets" or the "formula" used to calculate them. They are listed at the end of this chapter.

HOW THE CELLULAR RADIO SYSTEM WORKS

When a cellular system is installed, two separate licenses are issued by the FCC: one to an established telephone company, GTE for example, which is a "wire" system, and the other to a private company, such as Cellular One, which is a "nonwire" system.

The license allows each vendor to operate on a 10 mc.-wide band.

The nonwire channels start at 870.030 mc., and the wire system starts at 880.020 mc. Each channel is 30 kc. wide, which makes 333 channels each. They are arranged in 21 groups of 14 or 15 channels, and each group has one control or data channel.

The area in which they operate is divided into cells. Each cell has a main computer-controlled transmitter and receiver, and a secondary system goes in areas that have heavy use. Each cell computer system uses one group, and adjacent cells never use the same frequencies to prevent them from interfering from each other, although now and then, you may hear parts of another conversation bleeding over from another cell.

The cell computer systems, or sites, are about five miles apart, except in areas where there is heavy traffic or tall buildings and mountains, in which case they will be closer. San Francisco, for example, is 49 square miles in area but has seven sites that I know of. In San José, site 31A is in the 1900 block of S. Bascom Avenue, 32A is just a couple of miles north in the 3000 block of Tiche, near Interstate 880, and there are two sites in the Palo Alto/Menlo Park area, both near Stanford University, one of the most heavily used areas in the country.

Each vendor's system consists of the central office (CO), mobile telephone switching office (MTSO), cell sites, and mobile terminals (MT, cellular telephones).

The CO controls the MTSO, which controls the cell-site equipment, which control the MTs. When a cellular phone is first turned on, the receiver scans all twenty-one of the control or data channels, measures the signal strength of each, and locks onto the strongest one. This places the phone in that cell.

When the user makes a call and presses the send button, the number called and a series of codes are sent on the data channel to the cell-site computer.

These are part of the phone's number assignment module (NAM). Some of these are:

MIN: Mobile Identification Number, the telephone number assigned to the cellular phone.

ESN: Electronic Serial Number, unique to each phone. The EIAA interim standard, IS-3-B, defines the ESN: "The serial number is a 32-bit binary number that uniquely identifies a mobile station to any cellular system. It must be factory set and not readily alterable in the field . . . Attempts to change the serial number circuitry should render the mobile station inoperative."

Two to the 32nd power is 4,294,967,295, or 4.3 billion possible numbers. (The ESN is sometimes in the NAM or other chip or hidden elsewhere inside the phone.)

SIDH: System Identification Number, Home, which tells where the phone was assigned, its home area.

SCM: System Class Mark, the class and power output of the phone.

IPCH: Incoming Page Channel, the channel used by the phone to listen for an incoming call. The wire vendor phones use channel 334 and the nonwire use 333.

ACCOLC: Access Overload Class, certain phones have priority over others when the system is overloaded by too many callers trying to use it at the same time. The phones issued to law enforcement and federal intelligence agencies, emergency services, and the military have first priority: their phones can access the system when others are locked out. This number tells the system the level of priority the phone has.

PS: Preferred System, sets which of the two vendors the phone's account has been established on, wire or nonwire.

LD: Lock Digit, a feature that allows the owner to call his cellular phone from any other phone and enter a code number that will prevent it from being used should it be lost or stolen.

The computer reads the ESN and compares it with the MIN number to make sure they match, identifies the unit, and verifies that it is a registered unit, that the unit has not been shut off for one reason or another (reported stolen or bill not paid). Then the computer finds an unused channel based on the information received on the control channel and makes the call.

While this is happening, the computer is frequently checking the signal strength of the mobile unit. If the person calling is out in his car driving around, the signal will get weaker as he gets farther from the location of the cell's computer system.

If the signal strength falls too low, the mobile unit starts looking through the twenty-one control channels again, looking for a stronger one, which will be in another cell—usually but not always the cell that is physically closest.

If someone were listening on a scanner, he would hear a low buzz just before the channel changed.

Meanwhile, all that is happening on the control channels is being monitored by the main switching office, which controls the whole system (all the cells and all the channels for the vendor).

Then the switching office will locate a vacant channel in the new cell and send the mobile unit a code that causes it to switch to the new frequency. This is called "handing off."

When a call is placed to the MT, a page call is sent from the telco office to the MTSO, which sends it out on one of the two IPCH channels. The MT (if turned on) hears all these, and if it recognizes its own MIN and the owner answers, it responds by sending back its ESN. Then the MTSO selects a vacant channel and makes the connection.

If it is not answered, then the MTSO intercept recording comes on with a message such as, "The person you are trying to reach is not available," or "The cellular phone you are calling is out of range or is not turned on."

As long as a cellular phone is turned on, it is communicating with the nearest cell computer, and the system can tell where the phone is. In an area with many cells close together, such as a large city, it can locate the phone to within about a quarter mile or less.

The information that is passed back and forth between the MT and the cell site transceiver is called "capture voice channel assignment," and is in a frequency shift code called "Manchester."

The technical specifications for all this are found in *Recommended Minimum Standards*, publication EIA/15-3-B, available for $21 from the EIAA at 2000 "I" Street NW, Washington, D.C. 20006.

LISTENING AND TRACKING CONVERSATIONS

How well one can hear cellular phone conversations in general and track one in particular depends on three factors:

1. the scanner's quality and channel capability
2. The location of the listener and the antenna
3. How the scanner is programmed

There are a number of scanners available that work very well for cellular listening. One of the best is the AR-3000, which has a 1,000-channel capacity when interfaced with a computer. It can be programmed so that the channel sets are in separate banks, and the banks can be scanned in any order desired. The cost of the AR-3000 including the computer software is about $1300. The Realistic PRO-2006 is another good unit. Both are available from Scanners Unlimited and EEB.

The 2006 can have memory chips added to increase the number of channels to 1,000, which will cover all the cells for both vendors.

Whichever scanner you use, programming 333 to 666 channels into it means pushing from 3,000 to 6,000 keys, and one mistake can cause you to lose a conversation you would otherwise have been able to track.

LOCATION AND ANTENNAS

Obviously, you will hear more in a heavily populated area that in a rural setting. In the open countryside, there may be only one cell transmitter for several miles, but in big cities they may be only a mile apart.

No matter where you are, the better your antenna and the higher its location, the better reception will be. Using a good-quality coaxial cable and replacing it once a year or so also help. Scanner World, USA has a number of good antennas.

PROGRAMMING

How one may want to program the scanner depends on the area in which one is located and how many channels they have. Most scanners have ten banks, but there are twenty-one groups of cellular frequencies. Tracking requires the ability to switch

from one group to another as well as a good idea of which group to switch to.

Some of the twenty-one groups will be effectively out of range, again depending on the location, so ten banks are usually sufficient.

A way that one might start is to select a few channels from each of the twenty-one groups, program them into separate banks, and see how much action there is on each one.

People using cellular phones frequently reveal their location, so keep a list of those reported on each bank, and you will soon know the approximate location of the cell site. Also make notes on the strength of the signal.

After a day or so of listening, you will know which groups are the closest. Then program each set into one of the scanner's banks. This saves reprogramming over and over. This way, if you are tracking a particular conversation, you will have a good idea of which bank to switch to. If you know the general area of the phone you are tracking, when you hear the buzz, you will know the two or three scanner banks to activate.

A look at the cell layout diagram shows that when a phone leaves one cell, there are only six other cells it can move into, and knowing the direction it is moving narrows the possibilities to two or three.

Knowing the area also helps in tracking. If someone is following a conversation and the vehicle gets on a certain freeway, then he will be heading toward only one or two cells, and when the hand-off tone is heard, it is even easier to know which banks to activate.

If someone is serious about tracking, he should get a large map of the area, and after many hours of listening, he should be able to draw outlines of the cell areas.

MOBILE TRACKING

Besides tracking from a base location, one can follow a vehicle from a discreet distance and stay with its transmission, no matter where it goes. This can be done with a scanner, as in the base method, but a better way is to use a frequency counter.

Most counters, either portable or laboratory models, cover the cellular frequencies and will easily pick up the signal within a certain distance, depending on the type, quality, and number of other signals present that can interfere.

Typically, they will work from a few feet to 25 feet or so. However, there are preselectors that increase the sensitivity of the counter and, therefore, its effective range. One of the best, I think, is the APS104 from Optoelectronics. It will increase the range to some 250 feet, meaning you can lock onto a cellular phone from that far away.

Once you have the frequency, it only takes a few seconds to punch it into the scanner's memory or select the bank if it is already programmed.

A person interested in investigating someone could follow him around with a frequency counter and scanner to learn that latter's habits and routines, which yield a wealth of information.

• • •

The following page is a verbatim reprint of an article that I downloaded from a computer bulletin board.

WHAT YOU WILL HEAR ON CELLULAR RADIO

Early in the morning, the system is busy. You will hear people on their way to their jobs—doctors, lawyers, businessmen and women, and contractors. They will be calling their offices to check on their appointments, have their secretaries make lunch reservations, and the like. Sometimes they will be in a foul mood, and you will hear them badmouthing some of their employees or telling them to make up some excuse for them not keeping an appointment they want to avoid.

Sometimes big business deals are made, and people talk openly about how they are going to screw someone over or how something is about to come down on someone. People whose names you would recognize and events that could, and sometimes do, make the eleven o' clock news.

Later in the morning, the system is slower. Bored housewives call their husbands at the office, who often as not really don't want to talk to them because they are so busy.

The early drug deals start around noon, small dealers moving a gram of cocaine or a

half-ounce of pot, and business people squeeze in a few calls while on their way to lunch, the same bored housewives call each other on the way to the supermarket to get something for dinner and a bottle of white wine, and talk about charity events and going to the symphony to hear music they don't really like.

Late afternoon it gets very busy. Husbands calling wives to say they will be late because of this or that, or that they are just leaving the office and will be there in fifteen minutes, that they are hungry or horny, or in a bad mood, last-minute business deals and dinner reservations, people checking their voice mailboxes, salesmen calling in their orders, and the like.

Late at night it gets interesting. This is when the bigger drug deals are arranged. You will hear more people whose names you would recognize arranging to buy an ounce of coke or pot, crack dealers calling suppliers, pimps calling their "ladies" to see if they have been "busy" and sometimes threatening to come down on them if they aren't scoring enough.

People out partying call their friends to ask them to meet them at a nightclub or someone's home, people having a good time.

Sometimes you will hear people calling 900 numbers to talk about sex with $10-an-hour-convincing-but-bored women who pretend to care about the callers . . . people who are lonely . . .

Arguments are frequent, mostly husbands and wives or business partners yelling and sometimes making threats against each other.

Then early in the morning, it starts all over again.

• • •

Most of these people think, apparently, that their cellular radio conversations are private. Some of them just assume so, or perhaps have been told so by some person who didn't know any better. Many of them probably never really gave it much thought.

Some believe it because they were told so by the company that sold them their phone, either because the salesperson didn't know any better or because they lied to keep from losing a sale.

An executive of a company not mentioned in this book told me, "It is against federal law to sell a scanner that can receive the cellular radio frequencies." He seemed like he really believed this, but he should have known better. That company manufactures a product that is used in the cellular radio industry.

Perhaps if enough people exert enough pressure on GTE and the government, they will make the new encryption system available to the public. Until they do, I will not buy one.

THE CELLULAR RADIO FREQUENCY SETS

The first channel of each set is the data channel. The rest are voice channels. Some sets have a different number of channels. Each cell transceiver uses one set, and in some areas, a cell may have more than one transceiver.

The frequencies within one cell do not appear to change, although some people in the business claim that they do change, anywhere from every few seconds to weeks, depending on whom you ask. An executive of a company that makes cellular test equipment, not mentioned in this book, told me that they never change. My research indicates this to be true.

The cellular transceivers are duplex repeaters, and these listed frequencies are the repeater output that broadcasts both sides of the conversation. The mobile units are offset by 45 mc.

The first twenty-one sets are band "B," the wireline vendor. The second group of sets, band "A," are the nonwire vendor.

CHANNEL FREQUENCY		CHANNEL FREQUENCY	
SET 01		**SET 02**	
335	880.050	350	880.500
356	880.680	371	881.130
377	881.310	392	881.760
398	881.940	413	882.390
419	882.570	434	883.020
440	883.200	455	883.650
461	883.830	476	884.280
482	884.460	497	884.910
503	995.090	518	885.540

CHANNEL FREQUENCY		CHANNEL FREQUENCY	
SET 01 (cont'd)		**SET 02 (cont'd)**	
524	885.720	539	886.170
545	886.350	560	886.800
566	886.980	581	887.430
587	887.610	602	888.060
608	888.240	623	888.690
629	888.870	644	889.320
650	889.500	665	889.950
SET 03		**SET 04**	
343	880.290	352	880.560
364	880.920	373	881.190
385	881.550	394	881.820
406	882.180	415	882.450
427	882.810	436	883.080
448	883.440	457	883.710
469	884.070	478	884.340
490	884.700	499	884.970
511	885.330	520	885.600
532	885.960	541	886.230
553	886.590	562	886.860
574	887.220	583	887.490
595	887.850	604	888.120
616	888.480	625	888.750
637	889.110	646	889.380
658	889.740		
SET 05		**SET 06**	
340	880.200	351	880.530
361	880.830	372	881.160
382	881.460	393	881.790
403	882.090	414	882.420
424	882.720	435	883.050
445	883.350	456	883.680
466	883.980	477	884.310
487	884.610	498	884.940
508	885.240	519	885.570
529	885.879	540	886.200
550	886.500	561	886.830
571	887.130	582	887.460
592	887.760	603	888.090
613	888.390	624	888.720
634	889.020	645	889.350
655	889.650	666	889.980

CHANNEL	FREQUENCY	CHANNEL	FREQUENCY	CHANNEL	FREQUENCY	CHANNEL	FREQUENCY
SET 07		**SET 08**		**SET 11(cont'd)**		**SET 12(cont'd)**	
353	880.590	344	880.320	506	885.180	504	885.120
374	881.220	365	880.950	527	885.810	525	885.750
395	881.850	386	881.580	548	886.440	546	886.380
416	882.480	407	882.210	569	997.070	567	887.010
437	883.110	428	882.840	590	887.700	588	887.640
458	883.740	449	883.470	611	888.330	609	888.270
479	884.370	470	884.100	632	888.960	630	888.900
500	885.000	491	884.730	653	889.590	651	889.530
521	885.630	512	885.360				
542	886.260	533	885.990	**SET 13**		**SET 14**	
563	886.890	554	886.620	337	888.110	349	880.470
584	887.520	575	887.250	58	880.740	370	881.100
605	888.150	596	887.880	379	881.370	391	881.730
626	888.780	617	888.510	400	882.000	412	882.360
647	889.410	638	889.140	421	882.630	433	882.990
659	889.770			442	883.260	454	883.620
				463	883.890	475	884.250
SET 09		**SET 10**		484	884.520	496	884.880
342	880.260	348	880.440	502	885.150	517	885.510
363	880.890	369	881.070	526	885.780	538	886.140
384	881.520	390	881.700	547	886.410	559	886.770
405	882.150	411	882.330	568	887.040	580	887.400
426	882.780	432	882.960	589	887.670	601	888.030
447	883.410	453	883.590	610	888.300	622	888.660
468	884.040	474	884.220	631	888.930	643	889.290
489	884.670	495	884.850	652	889.560	664	889.920
510	885.300	516	885.480				
531	885.930	537	886.110	**SET 15**		**SET 16**	
552	886.560	558	886.740	339	880.170	345	880.350
573	887.190	579	887.370	360	880.800	366	880.980
594	887.820	600	888.000	381	881.430	387	881.610
615	888.450	621	888.630	402	882.060	408	882.240
636	889.080	642	889.260	423	882.690	429	882.870
657	889.710	663	889.890	444	883.320	450	883.500
				465	883.950	471	884.130
SET 11		**SET 12**		486	884.580	492	884.760
338	880.140	336	880.080	507	885.210	513	885.390
359	880.770	357	880.710	528	885.840	534	886.020
380	881.400	378	881.340	549	886.470	555	886.650
401	882.030	399	881.970	570	887.100	576	887.280
422	882.660	420	882.600	591	887.730	597	887.910
443	883.290	441	883.230	612	888.360	618	888.540
464	883.920	462	883.860	633	888.990	639	889.170
485	884.550	483	884.490	654	889.620	660	889.800

CHANNEL	FREQUENCY	CHANNEL	FREQUENCY	CHANNEL	FREQUENCY
SET 17		**SET 18**		**SET 21(cont'd)**	
341	880.230	354	880.620	502	885.060
362	880.860	375	881.250	523	885.690
383	881.490	396	881.880	544	886.320
404	882.120	417	882.510	565	886.950
425	882.750	438	883.140	586	887.580
446	883.380	459	883.770	607	888.210
467	884.010	480	884.400	628	888.840
488	884.640	501	885.030	649	889.470
509	885.270	522	885.660		
530	885.900	543	886.290		
551	886.530	564	886.920		
572	887.160	585	887.550		
593	887.790	606	888.180		
614	888.420	627	888.810		
635	889.050	648	889.440		
656	889.680				

THE 21 GROUPS FOR THE NONWIRE VENDOR

CHANNEL	FREQUENCY	CHANNEL	FREQUENCY	CHANNEL	FREQUENCY
SET 19		**SET 20**		**SET 01**	
				001	870.030
346	880.380	347	880.410	022	870.660
367	881.010	368	881.040	043	871.290
388	881.640	389	881.670	064	871.920
409	882.270	410	882.300	085	872.550
430	882.900	431	882.930	106	873.180
451	883.530	452	883.560	127	873.810
472	884.160	473	884.190	148	874.440
493	884.790	494	884.820	169	875.070
514	885.420	515	885.450	190	875.700
535	886.050	536	886.080	211	876.330
556	886.680	557	886.710	232	876.960
577	887.310	578	887.340	253	877.590
598	887.940	599	887.970	274	878.220
619	888.570	620	888.600	295	878.850
640	889.200	641	889.230	313	879.390
661	889.830	662	889.860		

The second column pairs for SET 01 and SET 02:

CHANNEL	FREQUENCY	CHANNEL	FREQUENCY
SET 01		**SET 02**	
001	870.030	002	870.060
022	870.660	023	870.690
043	871.290	044	871.320
064	871.920	065	871.950
085	872.550	086	872.580
106	873.180	107	873.210
127	873.810	128	873.840
148	874.440	149	874.470
169	875.070	170	875.100
190	875.700	191	875.730
211	876.330	212	876.360
232	876.960	233	876.990
253	877.590	254	877.620
274	878.220	275	878.250
295	878.850	296	878.880
313	879.390	314	879.420

CHANNEL	FREQUENCY	CHANNEL	FREQUENCY
SET 21		**SET 03**	**SET 04**
334	880.020		
355	880.650		
376	881.280		
397	881.910		
418	882.540		
439	883.170		
460	883.800		
481	884.430		

CHANNEL	FREQUENCY	CHANNEL	FREQUENCY
SET 03		**SET 04**	
003	870.090	004	870.120
024	870.720	025	870.750
045	871.350	046	871.380
066	871.980	067	872.010
087	872.610	088	872.640
108	873.240	109	873.270
129	873.870	130	873.900
150	874.500	151	874.530
171	875.130	172	875.160
192	875.760	193	875.790

CHANNEL	FREQUENCY	CHANNEL	FREQUENCY	CHANNEL	FREQUENCY	CHANNEL	FREQUENCY
SET 03 (cont'd)		**SET 04 (cont'd)**		**SET 09**		**SET 10**	
213	876.390	214	876.420	009	870.270	010	870.300
234	877.020	235	877.050	030	870.900	031	870.930
255	877.650	256	877.680	051	871.530	052	871.560
276	878.280	277	878.310	072	872.160	073	872.190
297	878.910	298	878.940	093	872.790	094	872.820
315	879.450	316	879.480	114	873.420	115	873.450
				135	874.050	136	874.080
SET 05		**SET 06**		156	874.680	157	874.710
005	870.150	006	870.180	177	875.310	178	875.340
026	870.780	027	870.810	198	875.940	199	875.970
047	871.410	048	871.440	219	876.570	220	876.600
068	872.040	069	872.070	240	877.200	241	877.230
089	872.670	090	872.700	261	877.830	262	877.860
110	873.300	111	873.330	282	878.460	283	878.490
131	873.930	132	873.960	303	879.090	304	879.120
152	874.560	153	874.590	321	879.630	322	879.660
173	875.190	174	875.220				
194	875.820	195	875.850	**SET 11**		**SET 12**	
215	876.450	216	876.480	011	870.330	012	870.360
236	877.080	237	877.110	032	870.960	033	870.990
257	877.710	258	877.740	053	871.590	054	871.620
278	878.340	279	878.370	074	872.220	075	872.250
299	878.970	300	879.000	095	872.850	096	872.880
317	879.510	318	879.540	116	873.480	117	873.510
				137	874.110	138	874.140
SET 07		**SET 08**		158	874.740	159	874.770
007	870.210	008	870.240	179	875.370	180	875.400
028	870.840	029	870.870	200	876.000	210	876.030
049	871.470	050	871.500	221	876.630	222	876.660
070	872.100	071	872.130	242	877.260	243	877.090
091	872.730	092	872.760	263	877.890	264	877.920
112	873.360	113	873.390	284	878.520	285	878.550
133	873.990	134	874.020	305	879.150	306	879.180
154	874.620	155	874.650	323	879.690	324	879.720
175	875.250	176	875.280				
196	875.880	197	875.910	**SET 13**		**SET 14**	
217	876.510	218	876.540	013	870.390	014	870.420
238	877.140	239	877.170	034	871.020	035	871.050
259	877.770	260	877.800	055	871.650	056	871.680
280	878.400	281	878.430	076	872.280	077	872.310
301	879.030	302	879.060	097	872.910	098	872.940
319	879.570	320	879.600	118	873.540	119	873.570
				139	874.170	140	874.200
				160	874.800	161	874.830
				181	875.430	182	875.460

CHANNEL	FREQUENCY	CHANNEL	FREQUENCY	CHANNEL	FREQUENCY	CHANNEL	FREQUENCY
SET 13 (cont'd)		**SET 14 (cont'd)**		**SET 19**		**SET 20**	
202	876.060	203	876.090	019	870.570	020	870.600
223	876.690	224	876.720	040	871.200	041	871.230
244	877.320	245	877.350	061	871.830	062	871.860
265	877.950	266	877.980	082	872.460	083	872.490
286	878.580	287	878.610	103	873.090	104	873.120
307	879.210	308	879.240	124	873.720	125	873.750
325	879.750	326	879.780	145	874.350	146	874.380
				166	874.980	167	875.010
SET 15		**SET 16**		187	875.610	188	875.640
015	870.450	016	870.480	208	876.240	209	876.270
036	871.080	037	871.110	229	876.870	230	876.900
057	871.710	058	871.740	250	877.500	251	877.530
078	872.340	079	872.370	271	878.130	272	878.160
099	872.970	100	873.000	292	878.760	293	878.790
120	873.600	121	873.630	331	879.930	332	879.960
141	874.230	142	874.260				
162	874.860	163	874.890	**SET 21**			
183	875.490	184	875.520	021	870.630		
204	876.120	205	876.150	042	871.260		
225	876.750	226	876.780	063	871.890		
246	877.380	247	877.410	084	872.520		
267	878.010	268	878.040	105	873.150		
288	878.640	289	878.670	126	873.780		
309	879.270	310	879.300	147	874.410		
337	879.810	328	879.840	168	875.040		
				189	875.670		
SET 17		**SET 18**		210	876.300		
017	870.510	018	870.540	231	876.930		
038	871.140	039	871.170	252	877.560		
059	871.770	060	871.800	273	878.190		
080	872.400	081	872.430	294	878.820		
101	873.030	102	873.060	333	879.990		
122	873.660	123	873.690				
143	874.290	144	874.320				
164	874.920	165	874.950				
185	875.550	186	875.580				
206	876.180	207	876.210				
227	876.810	228	876.840				
248	877.440	249	877.470				
269	878.070	270	878.100				
290	878.700	291	878.730				
311	879.330	312	879.360				
329	879.870	330	879.900				

FORMULA FOR FINDING CELLS

The following formula can be used to find all the frequencies used in a cell if only one of them is known and to convert between the frequency and channel number.

Frequency = channel number x .03 mc. + 870 mc.
Channel = frequency - 870 mc. divided by .03

For example, the frequency 880.050.
    Subtract 870.000

    —————————
    = 010.050

10.050 divided by .03 = 335.

880.050 is channel 335.
Reverse the formula, using channel 335:

335 x .03 = 10.050 + 870 = 880.050

If you hear a conversation on a frequency, use the formula to convert it to the channel number and find it in the list of sets above.

APPENDIX G
MODIFYING SCANNERS
FOR CELLULAR RADIO

THE REALISTIC PRO-2006

The Realistic PRO-2006 is available from Scanners Unlimited, EEB, and other stores that sell quality communications equipment, and it has excellent sensitivity and audio.

To modify it to receive the cellular band, remove the antenna and take off the top cover by removing the two Phillips screws of the top cover from the back. Looking at it from the rear, there is a metal plate that goes across the back of the front panel. On the left side, one corner of the plate is cut away. On the green circuit board behind it is a small screw, and below it are two glass diodes. Use diagonal cutting pliers and clip the wire on the bottom diode and then replace the cover. That's all there is to it.

This is what the newspapers call "very sophisticated equipment."

THE REALISTIC PRO-34

Modifying the Realistic PRO-34 portable scanner is not as easy as with the 2006, but it is not too difficult. You will need a small soldering iron.

Remove the battery holder, lay the scanner face down on your work area, and remove the four Phillips screws from the back. Inside the battery compartment on the bottom of the case are two small plastic hooks and a small paper label with a number like "7A8." Push out on that label with your thumb and the case will come apart.

On the back of the circuit board are four hex-shaped spacers that the four screws from the back cover went to. Use a nutdriver or pliers to remove them.

On the BNC antenna connector is a small bare wire that goes to the circuit board. Unsolder both ends. A second wire goes to the ground foil of the board from the outside part of the BNC connector. Loosen one end of it. (It may be a flat strip instead of a wire.)

At the lower left corner of the board is a small metal can about 1/4 inch square. It has a wire that goes to a small bracket. Unsolder it at the bracket end. Now remove the nuts that hold the volume and squelch controls to the top panel.

Just below the antenna connector is a row of small pins that project 1/8 inch or so. These pins are all that hold the two circuit boards together. Carefully, using a rocking motion, pull the two boards apart. The circuit boards used in the PRO-34 are thin and cheap and break very easily. Don't pull hard, just take your time and do it slowly, or you will ruin a $300 scanner.

As the two boards separate, work the volume and squelch controls from the top panel. Set the board aside. With the antenna connector at your top right, you will see a number of diodes on the left side. Clip one lead of the fifth one from the top. That's all there is to it. Now just reassemble it.

The PRO-34 is not one of Realistic's better products. It is cheaply made, and the one I used to have was not as sensitive as the Uniden scanners. It also does not have memory back-up batteries like the PRO-32, which means that if the batteries go dead, you have to reprogram it.

It also has an annoying beep tone when you use a 120-volt adapter and the batteries are not installed. The Uniden scanners are better and easier to modify.

THE UNIDEN 760 AND 950

To modify the Uniden BC-760-XLT and BC-950-XLT scanners:

Remove the four screws from the back cover. Locate the large Sanyo chip. It will have the number LC3517BM-15 printed on it, and it has thirty-two pins.

On one end of the chip is a small notch. With the notch at the top the pins are numbered from the top left corner, pin 1, down the left side and then up the right side; the bottom left will be pin 16 and the bottom right pin 17.

Pin 26 has two small traces going to it. Cut them with an X-ACTO knife and then carefully solder pins 26 and 27 together. Cool them with a damp sponge as soon as you are done. Integrated circuits are sensitive to heat.

Solder one end of a bare wire 1/2-inch long across pins 19 and 20 and the other end of the wire to the two traces that went to pin 26 before you cut them.

Now turn it on and enter a cellular frequency, and if you do not get an error message you did it right.

Listening to cellular phones is a violation of the Electronic Communications Privacy Act.

APPENDIX H
THE CELLULAR PHONE
NAM LAYOUT

CELLULAR SYSTEM DIAGRAMS

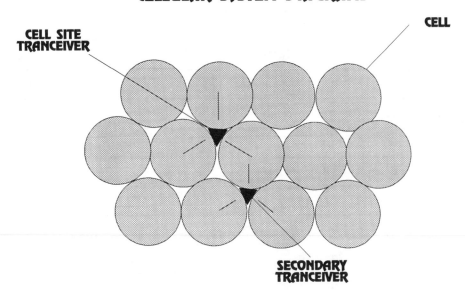

CELL SITE TRANCEIVER

CELL

SECONDARY TRANCEIVER

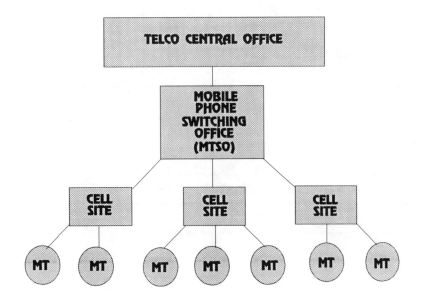

TELCO CENTRAL OFFICE

MOBILE PHONE SWITCHING OFFICE (MTSO)

CELL SITE

CELL SITE

CELL SITE

MT MT MT MT MT MT MT

THE CELLULAR PHONE 'NAM' LAYOUT

MARK DEFINITION	most BIT SIGNIFICANCE least	Hex address
	0 SIDH (14-8)	00
	SIDH (7-0)	01
LU=Local use	LU | 0 0 0 0 0 0 | MIN	02
	0 0 MIN2 (33-28)	03
	MIN2 (27-24) | 0 0 0 0	04
	0 0 0 0 | MIN1 (23-20)	05
	MIN1 (19-12)	06
	MIN1 (11-4)	07
	MIN1 (3-0) | 0 0 0 0	08
	0 0 0 0 | SCM (3-0)	09
	0 0 0 0 0 | IPCH (10-8)	0A
	ICPH (7-0)	0B
	0 0 0 0 | ACCOLC (3-0)	0C
PS=Perf Syst	0 0 0 0 0 0 0 | PS	0D
	0 0 0 0 | GIM (3-0)	0E
	LOCK DIGIT 1 | LOCK DIGIT 2	0F
	LOCK DIGIT 3 | LOCK SPARE BITS	10
EE=End/End	EE | 0 0 0 0 0 0 | REP	11
REP=Reprity	HA | 0 0 0 0 0 0 | HF	12
HF=Handsfree HA=Horn Alt	Spare Locations (13-1D) contain all 0's	13 to 1D
	NAM CHECKSUM ADJUSTMENT	1E
	NAM CHECKSUM	1F

APPENDIX I

GLOSSARY

AC: Alternating current. A current that reverses directions. It starts at zero volts, flowing from plus to minus, builds up to a peak (i.e., the 120 volts used in lighting circuits) then goes back to zero, and builds again to a peak, in the opposite direction, from minus to plus. This is one cycle. The number of times a second it does this is its frequency. House current, for example, is 60 cycles (per second).

ALLIGATOR CLIPS: Small spring-loaded clips made for temporary connections, such as to a phone line. This is a small version of the ones used on automobile jumper cables.

AM: Amplitude Modulation, an RF signal that uses changes in its amplitude (intensity or power, sort of) to carry intelligence.

ANI: Automatic Number Identification. A special, proprietary telco phone number that, when called, will answer with a computer synthesized voice that gives the number from which the call is placed. This is how telco employees, or anyone who has the ANI numbers, can identify an unknown line. A spy could use ANI from a telephone pole, or by tapping a multiline cable in an office building, to find the target line.

ANTENNA: Anything made of metal that is used to radiate a signal and increase the range of a transmitter. The proper length is shorter as the frequency increases.

ASCII: The American Standard Code for Information Interchange. Used in computer data storage and transmission, it has a series of eight ones and zeros used for numbers and letters.

AUTOVON: A phone system used by the military that has four DTMF tones that Touchtone pads can generate but are not included in other telephones.

BABY MONITOR: A type of wireless monitoring device that can use the subcarrier technique or can be an RF device.

BANDWIDTH: The width of a transmitted RF signal. For example, most two-way radios have a signal that is 5,000 cycles (5 kilocycles) wide. TV stations transmit a signal that is 6 megacycles wide. It occupies that much of the radio spectrum. TV channel 2 is from 54 to 60 mc.

BASE BAND: A signal output from a satellite TV receiver that can be used with a shortwave radio to hear satellite phone calls.

B-BOX or BRIDGING BOX: a large metal cabinet, usually on street corners, where the underground phone lines surface so telco workers can access them.

BBS: Bulletin Board System, or RBBS, remote BBS—a computer system accessible by phone using a modem.

BIAS: A weak signal generated by tape recorders to align the small areas of magnetism on recording tape, called domains, previous to sound being recorded. This signal can be detected by special devices made for the purpose.

BINARY: A system of counting using only the numbers 0 and 1.

BINDER GROUP (See also COLOR CODES): Telco uses these color codes to mark pairs of wires. There are two groups of five colors that can mark twenty-five pairs. Each bunch of twenty-five pairs is called a binder group and is marked using the same color code, to separate them from the other binder groups in a large cable.

BIRDIE: An internal signal generated by some scanners, which it "hears" as a station. It is usually heard as a low hissing sound. The newer scanners have eliminated most birdies, but all have a few.
To tell a birdie from a real signal, disconnect the antenna, and if it is still there, it is a birdie.

BIT: See computer terms.

BREADBOARD: A type of connection block used to design electronic circuits. It has rows of small holes that wires from electronic components can be inserted temporarily, eliminating the need to solder them and making for quick, easy changes.

BUG: As used in this book, any type of listening device. The term usually refers to a hidden microphone, alone, or attached to a radio transmitter.

BUG DETECTOR: A device used for finding an RF bug by tuning in on the signal it transmits.

BUMPER BEEPER: A small transmitter hidden in or on a vehicle, which transmits a beep tone and is received by a receiver made for that purpose, allowing the operator to track the vehicle.

BURST: A transmitter that converts sound to digital form, stores it, and then transmits it in a fraction of a second burst. This makes it more difficult to find with electronic equipment.

BYTE: See computer terms.

CABLE: Any number of electrical wires together inside an insulating sheath. It may contain from two to hundreds of wires.

CALL BLOCKING: A feature of Caller ID, in which you can prevent a number you are calling from knowing your number by dialing a three-digit code before you place the call. The person you are calling has the option of refusing calls that are blocked. Call Blocking will not prevent anyone you call from using Call Return or Call Trace.

CALL TRACE: Another feature of Caller ID, this allows the telco to determine the number of the last phone that called you, if you request it. However, the telco will not give you this information, only the police. Like an instant pen register, it is useful in trapping prank callers.

CALLER ID: A new system being offered by the Bell system. A small device attached to your phone will display after the first ring the number of anyone who calls you. It is available only in certain areas for personal phones, but is already in use on all 800 and 900 numbers. Any time you call one of these numbers, they have a record of your number.

CALL RETURN: A function of Caller ID that allows you to call back the last person who called your phone, even if you didn't answer.

CAMA: Centralized Automatic Message Accounting. A feature of the telco ESS that makes a computer record of all local and long-distance calls and stores them on magnetic tape. It is theoretically "for statistical purposes only" but is available to law-enforcement agencies.

CAPACITOR (also called CONDENSER): An electronic component that stores electricity in a DC circuit, and in AC it causes capacitive reactance to the flow of current, like AC resistance, sort of.

CARBON MICROPHONE: A microphone that uses small carbon granules inside a diaphragm. As sound enters, it vibrates the carbon, which changes its resistance, and these changes are heard by a telephone receiver as sound. It requires a DC voltage to make it work, which is why phone lines have DC on them.

CARRIER: An RF signal from a transmitter. It can have intelligence inside it (voices, music, etc.), which is separated by a detector.

CCIS: Common Channel Interoffice Signaling. Part of the new ESS used by telco to defeat phreakers. The dialing tones are sent over a separate line (loop) instead of the voice line.

CELL: A physical area that the cellular radio is divided into. Each cell has one or more computer-controlled transceivers. This is also a place where people can be caged for illegal surveillance. A cell may have a "window," depending on the jailer.

CNA: Central names and addresses. A division of the telco that maintains records of customers, which can be accessed by anyone who knows the numbers and terminology.

COCOTS: Company-Owned, Coin-Operated Telephone System. Privately owned pay phones. Generally easier to phreak than fortresses.

COLOR CODE: A set of colors used in phone wiring to identify the various pairs. It uses the colors blue, orange, green, brown, slate and white, red, black, yellow, and violet. Each pair (line) uses one color from each of the two groups.

COMPUTER TERMS: The following terms make it easier to understand the chapters on data encryption, but otherwise they are as boring to most readers as they were to me in college—in spite of an excellent instructor.

A computer stores data in binary form, which is a series of ones and zeros, a system of counting based on 2 instead of 10. Each one or zero is called a bit.

In a computer memory chip, each bit of information is stored as a low-voltage level, which can be a zero or a high-voltage level

(about 5 volts) which is a one.

Letters and numbers are made up of bytes, and a byte is made of eight bits. A letter would be stored as one byte or eight bits and so would be something like 10001011 or 01110101.

In data encryption, the DES, the data to be scrambled, flows into the program (in the original 64-bit DES) 8 bytes or 64 bits at a time.

These 64 bits are then rearranged, substituted, and transposed according to a prearranged plan, which is the key.

CONTACT MICROPHONE: A special microphone used to pick up physical vibrations, such as from a wall. Sometimes called an electronic stethoscope.

CROSSBAR: A type of telco switching system that was used to connect phone lines together. It used mechanical relays and has been replaced by the ESS in all but a few small telcos.

CYCLE: The number of times per second an alternating current reverses and changes direction. It is also called hertz.

DECIBEL: A unit used to measure the relative strength of an audio or RF signal.

DEMODULATOR: A circuit that extracts the intelligence from a radio or TV signal. It is also called a detector.

DEMON DIALER: See WARGAMES.

DES: The Data Encryption Standard, an encryption program written by IBM for the National Bureau of Standards.

DIODE: An electronic part similar to a transistor, except that it usually has only two layers of silicon instead of three.

DIP: Dual Inline Package, the plastic or ceramic material with two rows of pins that integrated circuits are built into.

DIP SWITCH: A small package the same size as

a DIP that contains a number of small slide switches, usually four or eight, and is about 1-inch long and 1/4-inch wide.

DIRECT LISTEN: An eavesdropping method using either a hidden microphone or a phone tap, in which wires lead directly to the listening post.

DISTRIBUTION CLOSET: A place, usually a small, locked room, where the phone lines enter a building and are connected to the various pairs of wires that go to the apartments or offices.

DOWN-LINE: Any place on a phone line outside the house or building, on a telephone pole, or in a telco junction point, etc.

DROP: "Make a drop"—plant, hide, or install a bug or listening device.

DROP WIRE: The phone wire that leads from a telephone pole to a building.

DTMF: Dual Tone, Multifrequency. The audio tones used in push-button telephones.

DVP: Digital Voice Protection, a secure method of scrambling radio telephone conversations. It is made by Motorola.

EARTH STATION: A satellite TV receiving system.

EAVESDROPPING: Any method, electronic or otherwise, of secretly listening to someone's conversations without his or her knowing.

ECPA: The Electronic Communications Privacy Act, a federal law that restricts which radio signals one can listen to legally, among other things.

ENCRYPTION: The process of scrambling letters to make them unreadable without the key or password needed to unscramble them.

ESS: Electronic Switching System, the computerized system the telco uses to connect one phone to another. This system replaced the stepping switches and crossbars.

EXTENDER: Term used for a line that can be used by phone phreakers to make phree calls.

FARADAY CAGE: A metal cage that uses copper mesh or other metal to keep radio waves from getting in or out, named after Michael Faraday, one of the pioneers in electronics.

FEDS: Generic term used here for federal agents.

FET: Field Effect Transistor, a different type of transistor that has a gate, source, and drain as its three parts.

FIBER-OPTIC: A thin glass fiber strand used to conduct light, which can be used in place of phone wires.

FIELD STRENGTH METER: An electronic device that detects the RF signals from transmitters, bugs, etc. It can be as simple as a small meter with a diode across it and a length of wire for an antenna, or a sophisticated and expensive type used by cable TV companies to detect cable leaks. The latter is made by Simpson.

FILTER: An electronic circuit or device that affects sound or RF signals that enter it. It can be used with audio signals to block out interference when used with a bug or shotgun microphone. The equalizer on a stereo system is a filter. Some types are:

- Bandpass—allows a certain range or band of frequencies (either audio or RF) to pass and blocks all others.
- Bandstop—the opposite of bandpass: a certain range is blocked, all others pass.
- T-notch—an adjustable filter that can be tuned to block certain frequencies, like an adjustable bandpass filter.

FLOOR CLOSET: A smaller telephone line distribution closet on some or all floors of office and apartment buildings.

FM: An RF signal that uses a change in frequency to carry intelligence.

FORTRESS: A pay telephone owned by Bell.

FREEWARE: Computer software made available to the public by the author without charge.

FREQUENCY COUNTER: A device that measures the frequency of a radio transmitter and displays it on the front panel.

FREQUENCY HOPPING: The technique of changing frequencies quickly to prevent the transmission from being intercepted. The Secret Service, for example, has 16 channels set aside for this, starting at 408.625 and including every 25 kc. up to 409.000 mc.

GATLING GUN: A type of shotgun microphone using a number of small tubes to make it very directional. Named for the Gatling gun, one of the first machine guns, which it slightly resembles. For details see *The Big Brother Game* by Scott French.

GIGACYCLE: Gc., a billion cycles per second, also called gigahertz.

GOLD BOX: A device for call forwarding, used before the telco had this feature. It requires two lines and can be used as an alibi for people to "prove" that they were home at a certain time. The person calls in on one line and makes a call through the other line. Since the telco keeps a record of all calls, it will show that a call was, indeed, made from that line at the time. The Gold Box can also be used as a remote-control phone tap by connecting it to the target line.

GROUND DETECTION: A system used in pay phones to prevent using a red box to obtain phree calls. It physically senses coins being dropped into the phone but does not count how many. To defeat this, the phreaker first drops a few coins in so the ground detection system will be fooled and then uses the red box.

HACKER: One who breaks into computer systems or telephone systems, voice mailboxes, answering machines, etc. It can also mean a person who has knowledge of computer hardware. The definition depends on whom you ask.

HARDWARE: The physical, mechanical parts of a computer—the circuit boards, disk drives, peripherals, etc.

HARMONIC: A multiple of an RF signal. For example, a transmitter with a signal on one mc. would also transmit on 2, 3, 4 mc. (and so on). These harmonics are "suppressed" in the transmitter and are usually very weak so they don't radiate very far.

HARMONICA BUG: See INFINITY TRANSMITTER.

HAZARD: Term used in sweeping for bugs to mean any place a listening device could be hidden. possible hiding places, or hazards.

HERTZ: See CYCLE.

HEXADECIMAL: A system of counting used in computers, based on 16 instead of 10. It uses the digits 0 to 9 and the letters A to F.
Counting from 0 to 16 would be 0, 1, 2, 3, 4, 5, 6, 7, 8, 9, A, B, C, D, E, F.

HOOK SWITCH BYPASS: A switch that defeats or bypasses the cradle or hook switch in a telephone to turn on the microphone (make it hot). It is used with an infinity transmitter.

HOT MIC: A microphone that is turned on, usually meaning the one in a telephone that has been activated by a hook switch bypass.

IMAGE: Image signal, a signal received by a scanner that is on a frequency other than that the scanner is tuned to. It is complicated but similar to INTERMOD. The "sum and difference" frequencies are generated by a circuit inside the scanner called a "local oscillator."

IMPEDANCE: A combination of resistance and reactance.

INDIGENT: A term that describes some writers of books on the subject of electronic surveillance.

INFINITY TRANSMITTER: A device that activates the microphone inside a telephone from a remote location, allowing the user to listen to the sounds in the room where the bugged phone is located. It was once called a harmonica bug.

INFRARED TRANSMITTER: A listening device that uses invisible infrared light to transmit intelligence, much like a TV remote control, except that little about TV is intelligent.

INTELLIGENCE: Generic term for information.

INTERCEPT: To overhear in any of several ways sound or video without the subject's being aware that it is being done.

INTERMOD: Intermodulation. This occurs when you hear a station on your scanner that isn't supposed to be there. When two RF signals combine in space, they mix together and produce the "sum and difference" frequencies of both. For example, station A has its signal on 10 mc., and station B is transmitting on 15 mc. If they are physically close to each other, the signals will mix and generate signals at 25 mc. (sum) and 5 mc. (difference), which can be picked up on scanners. Intermod signals are weak and have short range but cause some interference in large urban areas. Voice and beeper pager systems are the main cause of intermod because they have high-power signals and there are so many of them. More information about sum and difference frequencies can be found in books on the Fourier series, which were written for the purpose of confusing second-year electronics students.

JAMMER or USS JAMMER: A device that generates ultrasonic sound (USS), which causes most microphones to vibrate or oscillate and makes them deaf.

JUNCTION POINT: An underground room, usually entered through a manhole cover (personhole cover?) where telco lines are accessed for splicing and repairs.

KILOCYCLE: Kc., 1,000 cycles, also called kilohertz.

LASER: Acronym for Light Amplification by the Stimulated Emission of Radiation.

LIGHT MODULATOR: A device that causes sound in the target area to flicker the light from an ordinary lamp. The variations in light are converted back into sound at the listening post.

LINE-POWERED: A phone bug that draws power from the phone line and needs no battery.

LISTEN DOWN AMPLIFIER: Any audio amplifier connected to a phone line. It allows the user to hear anything on the line without seizing it (the phone is still "on hook"). If an infinity transmitter is on the line, you will hear the sound it is picking up through the amplifier.

LISTENING POST: Any place used to hear intercepted information. It can be on the premises, in another apartment or office, in a van parked nearby, etc.

LOJACK: A company that makes a special type of bumper beeper transmitter, used for tracking stolen cars.

LOOP: A special, proprietary phone number used in testing lines and such. If two people call the pair of numbers assigned to the loop, they are connected. Examples of loop numbers are: 415-923-9900 and 923-9901. These are old, no longer used.

MANCHESTER: A type of frequency shift code used in cellular radio to transmit the various numbers in the phone's NAM.

MDT: Mobile Data Terminal, sometimes called Mobile Communications Terminal (MCT). A computer terminal installed in a police vehicle that communicates with the base unit by radio. They use an unknown type of code, and no one we know of has been able to break it yet. It is digital and probably encrypted with the DES, which, for all practical purposes, makes it unbreakable.

MEGACYCLE: Mc., a million cycles per second, also called megahertz.

MODEM: Acronym for modulator-demodulator, a device used to convert computer data into sound so it can be sent through the phone lines.

MT: Mobile Terminal, a cellular phone.

MTSO: Mobile Telephone (cellular radio) Switching Office.

MULTIPLEXING: "Many into one," the technique of sending many signals through one wire or cable or fiberoptic strand. There are two methods. In frequency multiplexing, such as cable TV, each signal (channel) has its own frequency. In time multiplexing, each signal, such as a phone conversation, is sampled; a small part of it, a few thousandths of a second, is sent over the line; then the same thing with the next conversation. At the other end, they are recombined by a device called a demultiplexer.

NONLINEAR JUNCTION DETECTOR: An electronic device used for finding bugs by flooding the area with microwaves.

NAM: Number Assignment Module, the chip in a cellular phone that contains various numbers described in Appendix F.

OSCILLOSCOPE: An electronic device that displays electrical signals voltage, etc., on a screen. The squiggly lines on the introduction to "The Outer Limits" TV program were an oscilloscope screen.

OMNIBUS: The Omnibus Crime Control and Safe Streets Act of 1968, a long, complex federal law that concerns surveillance, among other things. It was written to control organized criminals and to confuse everyone else.

OUTSIDE EXTENSION: An extension phone at a different location, such as a second office, or an extension of a business phone at home.

PAIR: Name used for the two wires used by a single-line phone.

PABX: Private Automatic Branch Exchange, a private interoffice telephone system used in businesses and factories, etc.

PBX: Private Branch Exchange, an older manu-

al-type of PABX device.

PARABOLIC MICROPHONE: A disk-shaped device used to concentrate sound. See SHOTGUN MICROPHONE.

PARITY: As used in the section on data encryption, it is a system of checking computer data for errors. When data is transmitted—for example, over a phone line—it is sent in binary form. Each letter and number is 1 byte, which is 8 bits (see computer terms), but numbers and letters actually only use 7 of the 8 bits. The eighth one is sometimes used for parity. Parity can be even or odd (as set by the transmitting computer). Using odd parity, the program counts the number of ones used in the letter being transmitted, and if this is an even number, it adds a one in the unused eighth place (bit) to make it an odd number. At the receiving end, the computer counts the number of "ones" in each letter, and if it is not an odd number, then it knows that a mistake has been sent. Simple, no?

PEN REGISTER: A device used by the telco to maintain a record of all calls made to, or from, a particular number, also called a trap. It can be activated by programming the telco computer, and it can be used to trap prank callers, either by the recipient of the calls or by law enforcement. Before Omnibus there was no law prohibiting the use of them by law enforcement or whomever else. Now a court order is required. See also CAMA.

PENETRATE: To physically enter the target area to place a listening device.

PHONE TAP: Connection of a wire to a phone line or placement of a coil of wire on or near a phone or the line to intercept phone conversations. A tap can be series or parallel.

PHOTOCELL: An electronic component that changes light into electrical energy. It is used in solar-powered electronic devices such as calculators and can be used to power bugs.

PHYSICAL SEARCH: The process of physically searching for listening devices.

PICK: A device used to open locks when no key is available. They come in various shapes, such as ball, diamond, curved, and rake. For more information and illustrations of the actual size and shape of picks, see *The Big Brother Game* by Scott French.

PIRATE BOARD: A computer bulletin board that has stolen calling card numbers, pirated commercial software, telco confidential info, or other such information. Up front, they seem like ordinary systems, but they have secret codes that can be used to access hidden information. These access codes are passed only in person to trusted users.

POCKET DIALER: A pocket-size device that stores the Touch Tones of phone numbers in memory chips. It can be modified to make the sounds of coins dropping into a pay phone and used by phreakers to make free long-distance calls. See RED BOX.

POTENTIOMETER: A variable resistor such as the volume control in a radio or TV.

PROFILE: The composite information one can obtain about a person who has placed a listening device, using various facts such as the type of bug used, where it was placed, etc.

PROPAGATION: The way radio and TV signals act—how they are affected by objects in their paths, sunspots, or other signals. This is very difficult to understand, as radio waves are unpredictable at very high frequencies such as UHF.

PUBLIC KEY: See RSA.

RADIO SPECTRUM: The part of the electromagnetic spectrum where RF transmitters operate.

REACTANCE: The effect that certain electronic components have on the flow of alternating current. It can be capacitive, from a capacitor; inductive, from an inductor (coil of wire); or both. Reactance and resistance together are impedance, sort of like AC resistance.

RECTIFIER: An electronic device that changes AC to DC. AC flows in two directions; DC in only one. A rectifier allows the incoming AC to flow in only one direction. A diode is a rectifier, as are some vacuum tubes.

RED BOX: A portable device used to cheat pay phones by duplicating the sounds of coins dropping. In spite of the telco's efforts to stop this, this device still works.

REFLECTOMETER: Literally, to measure (meter) a reflection. A very sophisticated device that measures the distance to a break or tap of a phone line or cable by sending a signal through the line and measuring changes in the return (reflected) signal.

REMOBS: Remote Observance. An alleged method of telephone surveillance that uses one phone line to tap another from a remote location. The phone companies deny that it can be used this way. I believe that it can, based on personal experience, but this is only my opinion.

REMOTE-CONTROL BUG: An RF bug that can be turned on and off from a remote location. This makes it harder to find and conserves batteries.

REMOTE LISTEN: Using a radio or light transmitter to send the signal from a bug to a remotely located listening post.

REPEATER: A system that uses a larger, higher-power transmitter to relay the signal from a smaller one, increasing the range. Also an amplifier used to boost signals on long telephone lines.

RESISTANCE: The opposition to the flow of direct electric current (DC) in a wire or other conductor, measured in ohms.

RESISTOR: An electronic component filled with ohms that resist the flow of current. Usually made of carbon, turns of small wire, or a metal film.

RF: Radio frequency.

ROOM GUARD: A device used to detect an RF bug when it is brought into the area it is placed in.

RSA: The most secure computer data encryption program there is, also known as the public key system. It is named after the three Harvard professors who wrote it, Drs. Rivest, Shamir, and Adleman. Used with a long key, it is unbreakable even by the fastest computers.

SAM: System Access Monitor, an electronic device that reveals on the front panel the numbers contained in the NAM chip of a cellular phone by detecting its radio signal.

SEIZING: Answering a phone line and causing it to appear busy or in use, an off-hook condition.

SELECTIVITY: A receiver's ability to tune in one station without hearing another on a close frequency, to separate one station from another.

SHAREWARE: Computer programs that are sold at low cost (usually less than $5) on a trial basis. If the user decides to keep it, he is to pay the author of the program a registration fee, usually modest. Some shareware programs are better than commercial software that costs ten to twenty times as much. A good example is the database PC File, available from Buttonware in Seattle.

SHOTGUN MICROPHONE: A special housing used with a microphone to concentrate sound to enable it to hear distant conversations.

SILVER BOX: A modified Touch Tone dialer that has the four pairs of DTMF frequencies not included in standard phones.

SIXTY-SIX BLOCK: An electrical panel used for phone wiring in some large buildings, named for its capacity of 66 phone lines.

SKIP-TRACING: The process of finding people or information that leads to finding people, usually meaning people who have skipped town.

SNR: Signal-to-Noise Ratio, how loud a signal is in decibels in comparison to background noise. A 30 dB SNR is "full quieting," and all of the signal can be heard without any noise.

SNUGGLING: The process of making a bug transmit near the audio part of a television signal. This makes it more difficult to find as the loud buzzing sounds of the TV signal hide the bug.

SPARK-GAP TRANSMITTER: A device that uses high voltage to send a signal through the air. Used for ship-to-shore communications in the early years of this century, it interferes with other transmissions on many frequencies.

SPECTRUM: See RADIO SPECTRUM.

SPECTRUM ANALYZER: A special radio receiver that displays what it is receiving on a video screen. It is useful in finding bugs.

SPSP: Single Pair Station Protector, a small block in a metal or plastic can that connects a single phone line, used in private homes and small apartment buildings. It contains fuses to protect the line and telco equipment from voltage surges.

STEPPING SWITCH: The first automatic system used by telcos to connect lines. Invented by an undertaker named Strowger in the 1890s, it used large, noisy rotating mechanical contacts operated by solenoids.

SUBCARRIER: The principle used in wireless intercoms to send audio through power lines. It is also a method of transmitting other information hidden inside a signal. Muzak, for example, is transmitted on some commercial FM radio stations, and Video-text (closed captioning and other information) is transmitted by some TV stations, hidden in the VBI.

SUBCARRIER DETECTOR: A device for finding a hidden subcarrier bugging device or receiving subcarrier signals on TV channels and FM radio.

SUBCARRIER EXTENSION: An extension telephone that uses the same method as the wireless intercom or baby monitor.

SVX: A more secure method of scrambling radio and radio/telephone conversations that uses the DES. The government uses it so we can't listen to its conversations on our scanners anymore.

SWEEP: Using electronic equipment to search for listening devices.

TARGET: The area to be bugged or line to be tapped.

TDR: Time domain reflectometer, an electronic device that finds breaks or splices in a cable or phone line.

TELCO: Generic term for any telephone company.

TELEMONITOR: A device similar to the infinity transmitter, except that it will not prevent the bugged phone from ringing.

TELETEXT: Information hidden in the VBI. It includes closed captioning for the hearing impaired, news, weather, sports, stock-market information, and more. A decoder to receive this is available from some TV dealers. Zenith makes such a decoder. An unconfirmed rumor is that the feds use teletext to transmit secret information to the local field offices in the nineteenth line of the VBI.

TEMPEST: Acronym for Transient Electromagnetic Pulse Emanation Standard, which has to do with the amount of radiation from a computer system. The details are classified by the NSA.

TEST SET: A special telephone used by telco personnel. It has two alligator clips to connect to the phone wires, and a listen-only mode, among other things.

TORX WRENCH: A tool used to open special "security screws" used on some telco connection blocks, TV cable converters, etc.

TRANSCEIVER: A transmitter and receiver built into one unit.

TRANSDUCER: A device that changes energy from one form to another. A microphone, for example, changes mechanical energy (the movement of the diaphragm) to electrical energy.

TRANSISTOR: An electronic component that consists (usually) of three layers of silicon called the base, emitter, and collector. This is a bipolar-type as opposed to a FET and was invented in 1947 by Drs. Bardeen, Brattain, and Shockley at Bell Labs.

TRAP: Name for a feature of the telco system computer that can make a record of all calls made to the trapped number, used to find prank or obscene callers. Same as PEN REGISTER.

TRIMPOT: A small variable resistor (potentiometer) that can be mounted directly on a circuit board. It has a small screw on the end to adjust it. A trimpot is much smaller than other types.

TROJAN HORSE: A bug placed inside something, then sold or given to the person to be bugged. The gift is usually something that plugs in, such as a table lamp.

TUBE MIC: A small, usually plastic, tube attached to a microphone, then inserted into the target area through a small hole, such as a wall plug, from an adjoining room.

TVRO: Television Receive Only, a satellite TV receiver.

VAN ECK: Dr. Wim van Eck, the engineer who developed the method of eavesdropping on computers from a distance.

VBI: Vertical Blanking Interval. A TV picture is composed of a series of lines "painted" on the screen. Some of these lines cannot be seen on your TV set; they are used for other purposes—the vertical "sync" or "hold," and for teletext information. Adjust the vertical hold until you see the black bar on the screen. In the top right corner on some stations, you will see a series of small black squares that flicker off and on. This is the teletext information in pulse-code modulation. The VBI is the period of time (interval) that these lines that make up the black bar are being painted.

VOICE MAIL DIALER: A computer program that dials phone numbers, looking for voice mail systems.

VOICE MAIL HACKING: The process of breaking into people's voice mailboxes. Computer programs such as "FHACK" find the systems and then hack the passwords. It is available free on some computer BBSs.

WARGAMES DIALER: As in the movie, a computer program that dials phone numbers, looking for other computers and voice mail systems.

WINDOW: That portion of the radio spectrum that is displayed on the screen of a spectrum analyzer, among other things. See also CELL.

WIRELESS INTERCOM: An intercom that uses the power lines to send the sound back and forth, instead of ordinary wires.

WIRELESS MICROPHONE: A small radio transmitter that was designed to eliminate the problem of long cords, used by entertainers. It is often used as a bug.

ZAPPER: My term for sending a high-voltage, low-current burst of electricity down a phone line to burn out a phone bug. Done the right way, it will do just that. Done wrong, it will damage the telco lines or equipment and result in your incurring the wrath of Ma Bell, which translates as all hell breaking loose.

APPENDIX J
SUGGESTED READING

The asterisk (*) indicates government documents, which are mostly on microfilm and available at all libraries that function as depositories of U.S. government documents. Some libraries have them listed on CD read-only memory (ROM) computer database systems.

"Advances in Electronics Threaten America's Right to Privacy." *Research & Development* (January 1986): 52.

"American Library Association Protests FBI's Attempted Surveillance of Library Patrons." *Publishers Weekly* (October 1987).

Andreassen. *Computer Cryptography.* New York: Prentice-Hall.

Athanasiou, Tom. "DES Revisited—Eight Years Later, the Question Persists: How Secure Is the Data Encryption Standard?" *Datamation* (15 October 1985): 110.

"AT&T Model 1620E Phone Uses DES for Cellular." *Electronics* (June 1986).

Bamford, James. *The Puzzle Palace: A Report on the NSA, America's Most Secret Agency.* Boston: Houghton-Mifflin. 1982.

Becker. *Government Lawlessness in America.* New York: Oxford University Press.

Bosworth, Bruce. *Codes, Cyphers, and Computers.* Rochelle Park, N.J.: Hayden Book Company. 1982.

Boynton, Peter. *The Eavesdropper.* New York: Harcourt Brace Jovanovich. 1969.

Brandenburg, Mary. "Are Your Premises Clean and Free of Bugs?" *Accountancy* (July 1986): 66.

Brenton. *The Privacy Invaders.* Coward-McCann.

Brown, Robert M. *The Electronic Invasion.* Indianapolis: Hayden Books. 1975.

Budiansky, Stephen. "Cheaper Electronics Make It a Snap to Snoop." *U.S. News & World Report* (18 May 1987): 54.

Buranelli, Vincent and Jan. *Spy/Counterspy: An Encyclopedia of Espionage.* New York: McGraw Hill. 1982.

Bush, John. "Fiber [Optic] Lines Can Be Tapped, but Insurance Is on the Way." *Computer Decisions* (1 July 1987): 14.

Butler. *The Spying Machine.* Severn House.

"Card-Carrying Readers." *New Republic* (25 June 1970).

Carter, Craig. "High-Tech Snooping: Privacy Laws Do Not Cover Car Phones or Databanks—Yet."

Fortune (14 April 1986): 89.

Church, George J. "The Art of High-Tech Snooping." *Time* (20 April 1987): 22.

CIA Flaps & Seals Manual. Boulder, Colo.: Paladin Press. 1975.

Cohen, Stanley. *Invasion of Privacy: Police and Electronic Surveillance in Canada.* Carswell Legal Publishers. 1983.

"CRT Spying—A Threat to Corporate Security?" *PC Week* (10 March 1987).

Cunningham, John E. *Security Electronics.* Indianapolis: Howard Sams & Company.

Dash, Samuel. *The Eavesdroppers.* New Brunswick, N.J.: Rutgers University Press. 1959.

"Defeating Ivan with Tempest." *Defense Electronics* (June 1983).

Denning, Dorothy. "Protecting Public Keys and Signature Keys." *IEEE Computer* (February 1983).

———. *Cryptography and Data Security.* Reading, Mass.: Addison-Wesley Publishers. 1982

Dewdney, A.K. "On Making and Breaking Codes." *Scientific American* (November 1988): 142.

Donner, Frank J. *The Age of Surveillance: The Aims and Methods of America's Political Intelligence System.* New York: Random House. 1980.

Electronic Surveillance & Civil Liberties: Federal Government Information Technology. Fountain Valley, Calif.: Eden Press. 1986.

"Emissions from Bank Computer Systems Make Eavesdropping Easy." [van Eck computer eavesdropping]. *American Banker* (26 March 1985).

"FBI Chief Disciplines Six for Surveillance Activities." *New York Times* (15 September 1988): 10N, 20L.

"The FBI Confesses [to Domestic Surveillance]." *New York Times* (17 September 1988): N14, L26.

Francome. *Eavesdropper.* New York: McDonald & Company.

Free, John, and C.P. Gilmore. "Bugging." *Popular Science* (August 1987).

Freedman. *The Right of Privacy in the Computer Age.* Quorum Books.

"Freedom, Privacy and the Retail Snoop-Tech Boom." *Washington Post* (3 December 1989): 4C.

French, Scott. *Big Brother Game.* Carol Publishing Group.

Garrison, Omar. *Spy Government: The Emerging Police State in America.* New York: Lyle Stuart.

Gleason, Norma. *Cryptograms and Spygrams.* New York: Dover Publications. 1981.

Halperin, Morton. *The Lawless State.* New York: Penguin Books. 1976.

Halperin, Morton, and Daniel Hoffman. *Freedom vs. National Security: Secrecy & Surveillance.* Chelsea House. 1977.

Harrington, Thomas P., and Bob Cooper, Jr. *The Hidden Signals on Satellite TV.* 2d. Ed. Indianapolis: Howard Sams & Co.

Heritage Foundation. Washington, D.C. "First Amendment Is Not Compatible with National Security." (14 January 1987).

Herrington, Donald E. *How to Read Schematics.* Indianapolis, Indiana: Howard Sams & Company. [Teaches how to understand electronic "blueprints," which is useful for building things.]

Hughes, John. "Russians Will Be Russians."

Christian Science Monitor (9 November 1988): 12.

Kahn, David. *Kahn on Codes: Secrets of the New Cryptograms.* New York: McMillan Publishing Company. 1983.

Katz vs. U.S. 389 U.S. 347 (1967). Available in any law library. [Relates to the Fourth Amendment.]

Keep It Secret: Low-Cost Countermeasures to Defeat Taps and Bugs. Videotape, 90 min. Boulder, Colo.: Paladin Press. 1990.

Kelty, Robert. *Government Radio Systems* [6th Ed. on local government]. San Jose, Calif.: Mobile Radio Resources.

Kimball. *The File.* New York: Harcourt Brace Jovanovich.

Kolata. "NSA to Provide Secret Codes." *Science* (4 October 1985).

Kuzela, Lad. "Mobile Phones Unsafe?" *Industry Week* (10 July 1985): 32.

Lapidus, Edith J. *Eavesdropping on Trial.* New Jersey: Hayden Book Company. 1974.

Lapin, Lee. *How to Get Anything on Anybody.* Boulder, Colo.: Paladin Press. 1987.

Lapin, Lee. *How To Get Anything On Anybody—Book II.* San Mateo, Calif.: ISECO, Inc. 1991. [Available from Paladin Press.]

Le Mond, Alan. *No Place to Hide.* New York: St. Martins Press 1975.

"Librarians Challenge FBI on Extent of Its Investigation." *Publishers Weekly* (8 July 1988).

Lieberman, Jethro Koller. *How the Government Breaks the Law.* New York: Stein & Day. 1972.

Linowes. *Personal Privacy in an Information Society.* U.S. Government Printing Office, Washington, D.C.

Loder. *Eavesdropping on the Echoes.* Luramedia.

Long, Edward V. *The Intruders: Invasion of Privacy by Government and Industry.* New York: Praeger Books. 1967.

McLean, Don. *The Spy's Workshop: America's Clandestine Weapon.* Boulder, Colo.: Paladin. 1989.

McNamara, Joel. "For Your Eyes Only," *Mac User* (September 1988): 250.

Meyer, Carl, and Stephen M. Matyas. *Cryptography: A New Dimension in Computer Data Security: A Guide for the Design and Implementation of Secure Systems.* New York: John Wiley & Sons. 1982.

"Mind What You Say: They're Listening." *Wall Street Journal* (25 October 1989).

Moran, William B. *Covert Surveillance & Electronic Penetration.* Port Townsend, Wash.: Loompanics Unlimited. 1983.

Morganthau, Tom, and Robert B. Cullen. "The Battle of the Bugs." *Newsweek* (20 April 1987): 18.

Naegele, Tobias. "Encryption Foils Cellular Snooping." *Electronics* (23 June 1986): 20.

"The NBS DES [National Bureau of Standards Data Encryption System]: Products and Principles." *Mini-Micro Systems* (March 1981).

Oberdorfer, Bob. "Bugged Moscow Embassy Might Be Sold." *Washington Post* (27 January 1989): A18, col. 4.

O'Leary, Meghan. "Computer Security Module Wins Government Approval [for Treasury Department Electronic Funds Transfers]." *PC Week* (29 August 1988): C6.

Portfolio of Schematic Diagrams for Electronic Surveillance Devices. Mentor Publishers. 1979.

Potts. "Emission Security." *Computer Law and Security Report #27.* 1988.

Public Law 99-508, The Electronic Communication Privacy Act of 1986, Title 18 USC sections 1367, 2232, 2510-2521, 2701-2710, 3117, 3121-3126. [Available at most public and all law libraries.]

Rawles, James W. "The Army Goes Cellular." *Defense Electronics* (February 1989): 36.

Rivest, Ronald. *The MD4 Message Digest Algorithm.* MIT Laboratory for Computer Science. 1990.

Scacchitti. "The Cryptographers Toolbox." *Dr. Dobbs Journal* (May 1986).

Schlesinger, James. "U.S. Envoy Confirms Soviet Bugging." *Christian Science Monitor* (9 June 1987): 1.

Serrill, Michael S. "The No-Man's-Land of High-Tech: New Devices Aid Police but Threaten the Right of Privacy." *Time* (14 January 1985): 58.

Smith, E.T. "How to Beat the Snoopers." *Telephone Engineer & Management* (1 August 1988): 100. [Security device to protect cellular calls.]

Smith, Ray. "Who's Solving the Cellular Eavesdropping Problem?". *Telephone Engineer & Management* (1 January 1987): 14.

Smith, Robert Ellis. *The Big Brother Book of Lists.* Los Angeles: Price Stern Sloane Publishers. 1984.

Smith. *Privacy: How to Protect What's Left of It.* New York: Doubleday.

Spindel, Bernard. *The Ominous Ear.* New York: Award House. 1968.

SpyCraft: Inside Secrets of Espionage & Surveillance. Videotape, 50 min. Boulder, Colo.: Paladin Press. 1989.

"State Senate OKs Delayed Wiretap Bill." *Los Angeles Times* (13 May 1988).

"Tab for Wiretaps High, So Are Results, Report Says." *Washington Post* (25 September 1990). 21A.

Telephone Taps & Room Bugs: How They're Done, How to Defeat Them. Videotape, 50 min. Boulder, Colo.: Paladin Press. 1990.

"Thirty Years of Wiretapping." *The Nation* (14 June 1971): 744-750.

U.S. Attorney's Manual on Electronic Surveillance. Port Townsend, Wash.: Loompanics Unlimited. 1988.

U.S. Congress. "Electronic Surveillance within the United States." [Ask librarian for microfilm document Y 4.IN 8/19:EL 2.]*

———. "Materials Relating to Wiretap Disclosure." Microfilm. [Ask librarian for document Y 4.J 89/1:100/11APP.4.]*

U.S. Consumer Product Safety Commission. Washington, D.C. "Consumer Product Safety Commission and EIA Alert on Cordless Telephones." Document Y 3.C 76/3:11-3 EL 2/2. [This is a consumer warning about eavesdropping on cordless phones; it is on microfilm and available at public libraries. Ask the librarian for A-G10379810.]*

U.S. Department of Commerce. National Institute of Standards. Federal Information Processing Standards (FIPS). Washington, D.C. *Data Encryption Standard.* Publication 46. (January 1977).

———. *DES Modes of Operation.* FIPS Publication 81. (December 1980).

———. *Guidelines for Implementing and Using the NBS Data Encryption Standard.* FIPS Publication 81. Washington, D.C. 1981.

"Van Eck, Electromagnetic Radiation from Video Display Units: An Eavesdropping Risk?" *Computers & Security.* Vol. 269, 1985.

"These Walls Have Ears." *The Economist* (11 April 1987): 49.

Westin, A.F., and M.A. Baker. *Databanks in a Free Society*. New York: Quadrangle Books. 1972.

"When Spies Go To Court." *Washington Post* (12 June 1983).

Wiggins, James Russel. *Freedom or Secrecy*. New York: Oxford University Press. 1956.

"Wiretaps in the Wireless Age." *Newsweek* (4 November 1985): 66. [Eavesdropping on cordless phones and electronic mail.]

Wise, David. *The American Police State: The Government against the People*. New York: Random House.

———. *The Politics of Lying*. New York: Random House.

———. *Politics of Lying: Government Deception, Secrecy, and Power*. 1974.

Wise, David, and Thomas B. Ross. *The Invisible Government*. New York: Random House. 1964.

Zimmerman, Phillip. "Proposed Standard Format for RSA Cryptosystems." *IEEE Computer* (September 1986).